W9-CES-583

Don Green

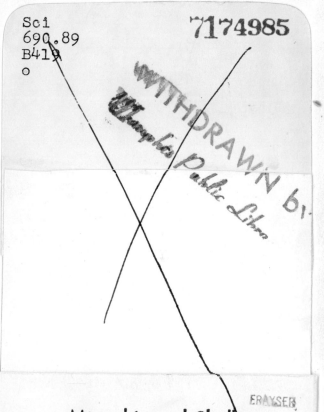

THE OUTDOOR
HOW-TO-BUILD-IT BOOK

Also by ROBERT LEE BEHME

Bonsai, Saikei, and Bonkei

Custom Car Annual Manual of Plastic Cars

Karting Ideas

The Official Automobile Handbook

1970 & 1971 Motorcycle and Trail Bike Handbook
(with Malcolm Jaderquist)

The Outdoor How-to-Build-It Book

by Robert Lee Behme

Photographs by the author
except as noted

A Helen Van Pelt Wilson Book

Hawthorn Books, Inc.
Publishers
New York

Designed by Harold Franklin

1 2 3 4 5 6 7 8 9 10

For my wife, Peggy

Contents

1

Containers, Hanging Planters, and Window Boxes

My first garden project was a simple planter of cedar, because it was not possible to buy a readymade one that was not decorated. I lived in a Los Angeles apartment, without workshop or tools, and bought my first hammer, nails, and precut lumber from a local supplier. The planter was assembled in less than thirty minutes and as long as my wife and I lived in the apartment it stood on the balcony, filled with fresh, green herbs.

Though gardening with containers is an ancient practice, there is seldom any look of antiquity in the styling of modern containers. They are versatile in both form and function, as effective on a roof garden or patio as beside a walk or drive. For portable color, I use low ones holding petunias and chrysanthemums and taller ones with oleanders for windbreaks. Some gardeners stagger several to direct foot traffic; others arrange groups of large ones for a measure of privacy. Whether you are a novice or an experienced craftsman, do try your hand at containers. Few objects are easier to design, simpler to assemble, or more useful, and nothing readymade quite equals the appropriateness of the custom-made. I have built hundreds. Although I give most of them away (they are welcome gifts), I keep many for our own use.

Design

Build without any special plant in mind if you like, but you will soon realize that the relationship becomes of basic importance. As a picture is to its frame, a plant is to its container: One must dominate, and the choice usually favors the plant. Not long ago I was asked to design a container for a Japanese laceleaf maple and after deliberation built a simple, undecorated wooden box. The container needed to be un-

1

obtrusive because the plant was bold, busy, and dramatic. When a plant lacks outstanding character, I let a fully ornamented container steal the show.

Consider size from two points of view. For form's sake, components should be agreeably related. Height, width, and length must balance visually. Second, the container must be right for the size of the plant. A small plant becomes insignificant in a large container and has too much earth around it to grow well. A plant too big for its box is as unstable and uncomfortable as it looks.

Let your container be of any shape that is pleasing in itself and related to the size and character of the plant and the surroundings. It can repeat, complement, or contrast harmoniously. When the height or symmetry of a tree is important, square and octagonal containers are best, but when the horizontal spread of branches dominates select oblong shapes. Simple designs are the most versatile but complex ones can be effective for a carefully chosen plant. I collect pictures of containers and adapt ideas from my files.

I think of small containers as less than a foot high. A 6-inch depth is the least possible for most plants. Such containers are easy to lift and facilitate a frequent change of arrangement. They are well suited to small terraces and balconies. The length of an oblong container is usually 1⅔ to twice the width—say, 15 x 9 or 16 x 8 inches. Square ones often have 10- to 14-inch sides.

In a garden you can use larger containers. Ideal for dramatic roles, their size demands a special setting—at one end of a deck or in the corner of an entranceway. I reserve such places for mine, often oversized boxes that hold one large shrub or a dwarfed tree. My wife appropriates the largest ones, 16 inches wide and 4 feet long, for masses of annual color. Since these containers are difficult to handle, I build wheeled platforms to make them mobile or I simply add four casters to a ¾-inch-thick sheet of plywood and slip this under the container. Sometimes I decorate the wood with tile or linoleum.

Materials

In time you will use a variety of materials—concrete, clay, even metal —but in the beginning rely on wood. As a material, it is the easiest to buy and use and ideal for outside planters. Wooden containers are easily assembled and require few tools. A saw, square, tape measure, hammer, waterproof glue, and rustproof nails will do for most jobs. If you own power tools, a table or radial saw, square cuts and mass production are easier, but hand tools will work. Cut all the pieces—

ends, sides, and bottom—before you assemble. Check each for snug fit. Then put the container together with waterproof glue and nails. On occasion, I build without preliminary plan, but when a shape is complex or the parts confusing, I plan each step on paper.

The base must be the sturdiest. Half-inch plywood is minimal, but when you choose conventional lumber, don't settle for less than 1-inch thickness. Larger containers usually require thicker woods. Quarter- or ½-inch plywood can be used for the sides of a small planter, but for a larger one, use ¾- or 1-inch material.

Plywood is excellent if you specify "exterior" or "marine" grades, which indicate that waterproof glue has been used and the wood is warpfree. Sheeting comes smooth or rough, finished or unfinished. Rough-cut plywood, sometimes called "re-sawn" or "rough-sawn," can be plain or grooved. Printed-grain plywoods are generally made in interior grades only, and so cannot be used near water, but when they are available with exterior glue, you will discover a range of attractive patterns.

Since artificial grains can be printed on various surfaces, a printed grain is sometimes considered to indicate poor quality, but this is not necessarily true. A hardwood with an artistic printed grain can be superior to a drab-yet-natural softwood. In addition, the graining process usually includes a coating that helps to seal and stabilize the wood's natural oil, prolonging its life. You may have to buy a full 4 x 8-foot sheet (enough for several containers), but occasionally a half or quarter panel is available. Most lumberyards will cut the sheet you buy into two or four pieces at little extra cost.

Solid lumber is my favorite. Cedar, redwood, and cypress are borer- and insect-resistant, important considerations for outdoor containers. Some other woods are nearly as good. Choose softwoods rather than hard. Pine and fir, for example, are far easier to work than oak. When you order lumber, remember that while plywood dimensions are "as advertised," conventional lumber comes in two measurements, rough and surfaced. Surfaced lumber is always thinner than the given dimensions.

The width of rough lumber may vary but the variation can be acceptable when accurate joints or cuts are *not* required. When accurate joining is needed, the lumber must first be squared. If you have power equipment, rip each board to a consistent dimension before cutting the finished lengths; if you have only hand tools, do not attempt this. Let your lumberyard do it; the service charge will be small. And if you'd rather avoid this sort of exchange, use "surfaced" lumber whose dimensions are consistent.

Lumber Dimensions in Inches

THICKNESS		WIDTH	
Rough lumber	Surfaced	Rough lumber	Surfaced
1	$2\frac{5}{32}$	3	$2\frac{5}{8}$
$1\frac{1}{2}$	$1\frac{5}{16}$	5	$4\frac{5}{8}$
2	$1\frac{3}{4}$	6	$5\frac{5}{8}$
3	$2\frac{5}{8}$	8	$7\frac{1}{2}$
4	$3\frac{5}{8}$	10	$9\frac{1}{2}$
		12	$11\frac{1}{2}$

Joining

Containers can be held together with screws, nails, glue, or any combination of these. Choose screws when holding power or durability is important and when you expect to dismantle the box later. Use long screws for maximum power, and be sure to predrill holes slightly smaller than the screws. Touch up with linseed oil to prevent rust.

Nails are a common choice, less expensive, easier to use, and satisfactory for most jobs. Combine nails with waterproof glue for permanence. Although steel nails work on most woods, choose galvanized to prevent stains and rust marks. With redwood, insist on galvanized, aluminum, brass, or cadmium-plated fasteners. Steel accelerates deterioration of wood. When nailheads can show, use less expensive box nails; when they must be hidden, use finishing nails and a nail-set.

Warping

The larger the container the greater the possibility of warping, but the danger can be minimized in several ways. An inside coating of wood preservative helps. Asphalt and copper are good, but I prefer fiber glass. An application of resin adds strength and makes a container waterproof. The ends can be secured on the inside, and below ground level, with metal L–braces; an expanse of sideboard can be supported with a bottom cross-brace screwed or nailed to base and sides.

Finish

The choice of finish depends on the wood, the design of the container, and its setting. Most woods can be left unfinished for a weathered look. Redwood, cypress, and cedar darken naturally to a beautiful silver gray. Their grain can be emphasized with a wire brush. The Japanese "burned" finish can be duplicated with a butane torch. The deeper you burn the more the grain is emphasized. The charcoal tone can be lightened by wire brushing.

Redwood and cypress can be treated with glossy or matte finishes. For an obvious gloss, use spar varnish or plastic "bar" finish. For less shine, apply varnish or shellac diluted with mineral spirits or thinner; for a matte surface, rub the wood with several coats of warmed linseed oil or linseed oil and turpentine combined in equal parts. Such a finish generally yellows cedar. When you need a truer tone, try a water seal, such as those made by Thompson and Behr or Jasco's Penta Five. Oil and varnish also yellow pine and fir, but the tones can be controlled with stains. Wood can also be painted to match or complement your house or any interior.

Containers can be "metalized" with thin sheeting. Household aluminum foil works well and is inexpensive; copper also looks nice. A copper-sheeted armored sisal-kraft does the best job. It comes in 6- to 36-inch widths and serves as a moisture barrier in many kinds of construction. Both materials can be cut with scissors.

On a rectangular box, wrap the four sides with a single piece, but on angled planters cut the sides individually. Don't glue the material, instead attach with matching aluminum or copper tacks. When two edges overlap, allow an inch or more extra so the edge can be doubled to look neat. For a hammered effect, spread the foil on a level board and tap it gently with a small ball-peen hammer before wrapping.

Plain containers have the broadest use, but even the simplest of these can be decorated if you wish. Thin wooden strips can be glued or nailed to the sides in linear and geometric patterns. Precut possibilities can be found at your lumberyard, such as scalloped wood designed to hold roofing tile. Metal ornamentation can be added with screws, bolts, or glue.

Interesting and useful items can be discovered in surplus stores and import outlets. Handles, from plain galvanized types to ornate Chinese cast-iron lotus blossoms, can be found in some cities, particularly in antique shops.

Make permanent containers first, because they are easiest. Once you've gained experience, try knock-aparts—planters whose sides are held together with rope, wire, or bolts. Such containers can be taken apart for root pruning and can be stored flat.

Square and oblong shapes are fastened with bolts. The end pieces are 2 or 3 inches wider than the distance between the sides, with two or four holes in the outer edges. Threaded bolts, 2 inches longer than the container, are passed through. Washers and nuts are added and tightened to secure the sections. Lumberyards and hardware stores carry the rods in diameters of ¼ inch or more.

Octagonal containers can be secured with rope wrapped around top and bottom. I drill holes in one side for each rope, bringing the ends inside and fastening them with galvanized staples. Octagonal containers are not difficult when you have a power saw. I set the blade at 22.5° for the proper bevel.

Display areas

Planters can be displayed against many existing backgrounds—a section of fence, part of a house wall, the sides of an entrance or wide stairs, or on a paved area. Or you may reserve a special place for important and changing displays. The simplest area is a gravel bed or a defined section of rock near the house. On either, containers become a point of interest.

Or you can make a low, portable display bench for them. To build a small one, cut six 24-inch sections of 1 x 1 and two 12-inch pieces of 2 x 4. Place the 2 x 4s 20 inches apart. Then, beginning at one end, nail the 1 x 1s to the larger wood with a 2-inch overlap at each end. Space the strips equally (2 inches apart).

To build a larger bench, cut the 1 x 1 material in 3-foot lengths. Add a third 2 x 4 to the center for support. Permanent platforms can be made of plywood nailed to a framework of 2 x 4s, or use 1 x 6 to 1 x 12 lumber the same way. Some gardeners build various-sized platforms that stack like bleachers for dramatic stagings.

Tall benches are made the same way as the seats described in Chapter 4. Use 2 x 4 or 4 x 4 support on concrete blocks to minimize the danger of dry rot and termites. Make the tops of 1- or 2-inch lumber, the size depending on the load carried and the unsupported length. If you build a series of benches of various heights, you can effectively display great masses of color. You can even create instant displays by grouping flats of annuals in bloom. To improve the plain flats, decorate them with collars of brick or painted wood.

Hanging planters

To fully enjoy trailing fuchsias, begonias, ivy, geraniums, and other pendant plants, show them at, or above, eye level. True, you can display them on shelves, but for a gayer effect, try hanging baskets. Baskets? Possibly so called because early kinds were entirely of wire, but many other materials are used now. Wooden ones are popular and can be built the same way as portable ground-level planters. Square and hexagonal shapes are obviously appropriate, but other shapes may be better for certain effects and situations. In any form they hold colorful flowers or foliage and often add a delightful vertical dimension.

There are a number of ways to suspend containers. Simple wire clips convert clay pots to hangers, and readymade supports do the same for wooden boxes, but I prefer the practicality of wire and chain, although rope is good for large planters. Supports can be fastened to a wooden container by three or four eye-hooks or -bolts. When the container is lightweight, I screw hooks into the sides; when weight is a problem, eyebolts through the wood offer greater security. Before attaching, try both at various points around the container to check for best balance.

You can connect separate wires from the hooks to the roof, but to avoid visual confusion, bring shorter lengths to a center point above the plant. Then run a single strand to the roof. When planters are hung in arbors, the chain or wire can be wrapped around an exposed beam; in other cases an eyebolt, through a solid timber or a screwed-in-place plate, makes a safer mounting.

Window boxes

With window planters you can bring color or greenery to long expanses on the outside walls of your house. Boxes can hold permanent year-round plantings or a collection of pots and other small containers for changeable displays. For either use, build as securely as you would any portable planter but with heavier lumber. Boxes must be well supported: 2 x 4s are the smallest, acceptable only for small types; 3 x 6 and 4 x 8 are best for large boxes. One support on each end is adequate for boxes shorter than 4 feet, but add one or two supports near the center for longer ones. Supports can be bolted to studs where the house studding is exposed. When it is not, nail the timbers through the siding into the framework with long spikes; provide heavy metal hangers or leg supports from the outer edges to the ground. As with portable containers, protect interiors with wood preservative or fiber glass. The exterior can be painted, stained, rubbed with linseed oil, or left to weather naturally.

Remember that while wooden containers retain moisture better than those of clay, concrete, or metal, plants in them still require regular care and more food and moisture than plants in the ground. The small amount of soil in a box is simply not adequate. Plants may also need pinching and pruning to look their best, for they are viewed from close at hand, and each one is prominent.

Of the various materials used for containers, plywood and conventional lumber are easiest to work and most adaptable. For plywood, insist on exterior and marine grades; only these are made with waterproof glue. Cut all parts before assembling any.

Bottom should be ¾ to 1 inch thick. Sides and bottom can be joined in several ways. Nails, screws, and waterproof glue are best.

Shell can be assembled before reinforcing corners. When nails are to be hidden, use finishing nails and a nail-set, which countersinks the heads. When heads can show, as in a rustic design, use less expensive box nails, but always galvanized to prevent rust and stains.

Reinforce corners for added strength. Metal angle braces are helpful on large containers. Wood is sufficient on small ones. Cut strips a little shorter than soil level and glue to four corners.

All containers need drainage holes, number depending upon size, but at least three. Drill holes before or after assembling.

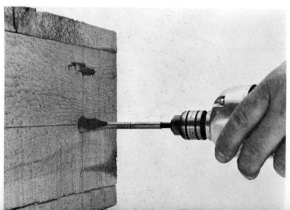

Attach feet to raise the base of the container. Elevated base allows air circulation and drainage. Feet can run across the short or long side, and should be proportioned to accentuate the design.

The dovetailed corners on this handmade box are beautifully made. They are secured by dowels that extend through the joints. Courtesy of Mrs. Emil Steinegger

Provide instant color with nursery flats of blooming plants. Protect the flowers with plastic while you spray the sides with paint. Two coats are usually required.

Or conceal the flat with a perimeter of bricks. If bricks need cutting to fit, use a hammer and chisel.

Simple containers made of 1 x 12 rough lumber, sized to hold two or three pots. Color and flowers can be changed quickly. Strybing Arboretum, San Francisco

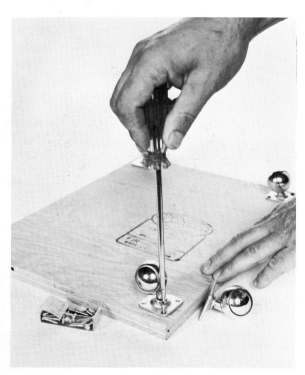

Improve the mobility of large planters with rolling platforms. Screw four casters to a square of ¾- or 1-inch plywood.

A movable platform decorated with a pebble and concrete mosaic. Polygonal planter can be knocked apart and then held together with rope in the top groove, or in top and bottom grooves for large planters. Marc Askew, designer

Simple display platforms can be made from 1 x 1 and 2 x 3 or 2 x 4 wood with thinner material for top slats, thicker for feet. Feet are inset 2 inches. Galvanized nails prevent stains and rust.

1 x 1s are spaced equally across feet. Use finishing nails for invisible joints.

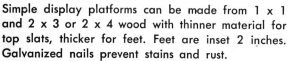

A finished slat platform. Casters give ready mobility. Tub planter was adapted from a pickle barrel. Marc Askew, designer

Wooden containers can be decorated in various ways. Here rope has been used, keeping the scale and the texture.

Containers that match the walk. The informal aggregate design adds a nice touch. Lawrence Halprin and Associates, L.A.

Commercial hangers for clay pots screw into wall and clip firmly to the pot. Inexpensive and available in several sizes.

An enthusiastic builder of containers may become a collector of handles. Flush handle, *upper left,* is made from deck latch. Cast-iron lotus design, *top,* and brass sun from import store. Antique handles, *left,* from junkshops and antique stores. Wooden handle is made to be painted.

An elegant planter decorates these patio steps. For a less formal effect wooden containers can be stuccoed, as is this one, the finish stippled or smooth. Strybing Arboretum. Thomas D. Church, L.A.

Long containers can be made to fit below windows. This one is decorated with horizontal slats to accentuate the length. Note the support cut to match the slant of the pavement. Los Angeles County Arboretum

Small trees can be permanently held, or displayed for long periods, in large containers. These are made of grape stakes and accord well with the surroundings. Braemar Homes, Los Angeles. Armstrong and Sharfman, L.A.

Ready-made containers appear custom-made when wooden feet of redwood are attached. The Japanese black pines were planted several years ago. Courtesy of Mr. and Mrs. Arthur Shapiro. Jocelyn Domela, L.A.

Hanging containers add a vertical dimension, and some plants look better when cascading. Plywood and 1-inch wood are good material. These hangers are rimmed with a well-spaced edge, giving a satellite look. Residence of Mr. and Mrs. A. Bloom. Armstrong and Sharfman, L.A.

Display areas for plants are where you make them. This is the top of a sundial. Garden of Dr. and Mrs. Francis E. Howard

Clay containers on a support made of laminated 1 x 12 lumber. Groups of five 1 x 12s are glued together, then joined with spacing between. The effect is that of a handsome butcher's block, rugged and in key with the setting.

Circular display platform built around a tree in a patio corner makes a focal point for seasonal color in clay pots. Garden of Mr. and Mrs. Harold Hecht. Jocelyn Domela, L.A.

Stepped display area effectively shows off many plants. Concrete footing keeps benches level, prevents sagging and dry rot. Benches are made of 6 x 6 timbers and 2 x 12 boards. Unfinished lumber is used for rustic effect. Courtesy of John Dutro

A raised concrete planter forming both a focal point and a major design element.
Mayfair Homes, Thousand Oaks, Calif.

A large concrete planter with a white cement edge is set against a brick floor.
Foothill Square, Oakland, California. Lawrence Halprin and Associates, L.A.

2

House Numbers, Mailboxes, Bird Feeders and Houses, Garden Ornaments, Pools, and Fountains

A Cleveland man once remarked, "My garden would be perfect with the right decorations, but I can't find them. I have to settle for second-rate stuff."

I had heard the complaint before. Gardeners across the country claim that they must choose commonplace objects because ornaments and accessories of character are almost impossible to find. And I tell them they're wrong. For one thing, beautiful old garden ornaments, or objects well suited to be so used, do appear in some odd shops or sales, though usually at prohibitive prices.

In my garden one-of-a-kind embellishments run the gamut, from bird feeders and concrete plaques to pools and fountains, and I have made or installed all of them. If you can hold a hammer or squeeze a tube of glue, you can do the same, and with great pleasure and satisfaction.

House numbers

New address markers put your best foot forward. Suburban and rural markers are commonly difficult for strangers to find, hard to read, and unattractive. A marker carefully planned for your entrance and situation will be highly visible, immediately legible, and inviting. You can make one in half a day.

Choose readymade or custom-made numbers. Their display is more important than their design. Fine calligraphy is seldom available, but conservative, mass-produced numbers are ubiquitous, and good if used with discretion. Or if you own power tools, a scroll, saber, jig or band saw, you can cut your own numbers. Either way, select styling on the basis of legibility. Simple numbers become focal points. Small or "artistic" ones get lost.

Nail the raised or molded numbers to a timber, and cast them in concrete. Mount the finished block beside the walk. Or nail each digit to a separate, short length of 2 x 4, then place the lengths together in the ground where they can easily be seen from a car. For permanence, use redwood, cedar, or cypress, with a concrete footing. Glue either type of number to a square of translucent plastic. Frame and mount beside the curbing. With a low-voltage light on one side the sign becomes conspicuous. For other ideas of what to do and what not to do, tour the suburbs of any city.

Mailboxes

Mailboxes of the conventional door-slot and the vaulted galvanized types are not the only possibilities. A variety of receptacles can be used, so long as you comply with a few basic regulations. Postal requirements are most restrictive in rural areas where the mail is delivered by car. Boxes there must be curb-side and car-height, since the driver is not required to leave his vehicle. If snow is a problem, the box must offset for the road plow as well. Box locations, dimensions, and heights vary and are determined locally by your postmaster and route mailman. Check for exact specifications with your postmaster. But if you want originality you must design it. Commercial boxes are all much alike, the ornamented ones worse than the plain.

Slots can be decorated to match or contrast with your entry, and boxes can be handled similarly. Use plastic, tile, metal, or wood. One man covered a ready-made box with a metal shell. Another used painted wood. Both boxes were mounted on special columns. Other home-owners build the entire container. Any well-balanced design is acceptable if function predominates. The construction can be simple, similar to that for the containers in Chapter 1 and for the birdhouses that follow in this chapter. Size is important only insofar as the box is large enough to accommodate a little more than the volume of mail normally received.

When several households receive mail at the same stop, the boxes can well be grouped on a common support. Constructing the unit would be a neighborly project. Use 4 x 4 or 6 x 6 uprights set in concrete, and add 2 x 6 timbers for cross supports. Mount the boxes on these and add a waterproof compartment below for packages. The receptacles could be either handmade or commercial boxes decorated or modified in an unusual way. For dignity and a sense of order they should be uniform. Planting will relieve the stiffness of the uprights. Where soil is poor or moisture low, container plantings are best, provided of course that maintenance is assured. The plantings can be changed from season to season, if desired.

A box can do more than hold mail. Add grillwork or a touch of color and it becomes a decoration. Add electricity and it becomes a path light. Add numbers and it becomes house identification.

Bird feeders and houses

Feeders and houses attract and hold birds, and nothing is more satisfying in a garden than their colors, sounds, movement, and excitement. Bird-lover or not, you will enjoy the sense of life and of nature that they impart. Mail-order equipment is available, some of it Audubon Society–approved, quite practical and good-looking; but in general, suitable items are difficult to find and it is far more satisfying to design and make your own.

The simplest feeder is a shelf tacked to a window ledge. My wife and I had one in our Los Angeles apartment and attracted hundreds of birds. A board 14 inches square can feed several birds at one time. To keep food on the deck, add a ½-inch lip. For all-weather protection, put on a roof—the Audubon Society recommends glass. To keep off cats and squirrels, suspend feeders by wires or place a 12- to 16-inch collar of plywood or galvanized metal around the post and under the feeder.

The first garden feeder I made was a 16-inch-square plywood platform, cat-free and squirrel-free because it was appreciably wider than its post. For weather protection, I added a roof and three glassed-in sides. The glass made the birds visible and showed when to replenish supplies. Later I mounted the platform on a pivot to increase protection from cold and rain. With fins on the open side, gusty winds swung the feeding end away.

Now we include suet cakes in winter, a combination of melted fat and seeds. I put them in feeders made from wire tacked to plywood backing. The feeders are placed on and against trees. We also make chickadee sticks, foot-long sections of 2 x 4 drilled with 1-inch holes. The holes are filled with suet mix and the sticks hung from limbs. Squirrels love the mix, too, and if you want it strictly for birds, suspend the sticks on thin copper wire at least 8 feet above ground and 10 feet from any overhead or adjacent branch.

More than forty species of birds will nest in houses, and three basic types will attract most birds: rustic, for woodpeckers; open-fronted, for mourning doves, robins, phoebes, and barn swallows; and enclosed, for many other species. The three structures should be scaled for one or two families, with the exception of the purple martin multiple apartments common in the East.

Use exterior-grade plywood or conventional lumber (¾-inch plywood and 1-inch boards are good choices), and design the houses for the birds of your locality. Requirements vary with each species, so consider these points: size of opening, floor space, house type, and height above ground. A 1½- to 2¼-inch opening is adequate for most birds. Wrens prefer 1- to 1½-inch circles; saw-whet owls, 3 to 3½. Barn owls, largest of the listed birds, prefer 6-inch holes. Other preferences are shown in the chart on page 21.

Many gardeners like birdhouses that are brightly colored. Others claim that only muted tones attract birds. A test was made at the University of Wisconsin. Identical houses in a range of colors were erected on campus, and students noted the number of times birds chose each house. Results indicate that color has only a slight effect. White, yellow, and blue were least popular, darker tones were most popular, but birds showed no preference between shades of green and red.

Ornaments

Ornamentation can translate the purely functional into something that gives a dimension, an accent, a touch of style to a garden. You can buy a considerable variety of statuary, fountains, and gadgets, but few are as attractive and appropriate as those you can make. Start with simple displays. Rocks and weathered wood are always interesting. Look for pieces that suggest other uses. A length of contorted wood can become a light standard or mailbox post. A large hollowed stone can become a basin. A group of rocks may be a striking abstract arrangement, may be piled and combined into a lantern, or in the Japanese manner suggest water where there is none.

The imaginative use of commonplace materials is especially gratifying. Flowerpots are amazingly convertible. Turn one on its side, add a candle, and it is a patio light. Turn another upside down, tie a short piece of metal inside, and the pot is a wind bell. Glue several pots end to end, and you've made a decorative column.

Wood seems to invite inventiveness. Several years ago I was given

Chart I   Birdhouses: Basic Specifications

SPECIES	FLOOR AREA IN INCHES	TYPE OF HOUSE	HEIGHT ABOVE GROUND IN FEET
Bluebird	6 x 6	enclosed	6 to 10
Chickadee	4 x 4	enclosed	7 to 10
Dove			
Mourning	9 x 9	open	6 to 13
Flicker	7 x 7	enclosed	11 to 22
Martin			
Purple	6 x 6	enclosed	12 to 22
Nuthatch	5 x 5	enclosed	11 to 22
Owl			
Barn	10 x 19	enclosed	9 to 35
Saw-whet	6 x 7	enclosed	12 to 25
Screech	8 x 8	enclosed	10 to 30
Phoebe	5 x 5	open	8 to 14
Robin	8 x 8	open	6 to 14
Swallow			
Barn	6 x 6	open	8 to 14
Tree	6 x 6	enclosed	9 to 18
Woodpecker			
Downy	5 x 5	rustic	12 to 25
Hairy	6 x 6	rustic	12 to 25
Red-headed	6 x 6	rustic	12 to 25
Wren			
Carolina	4 x 4	enclosed	6 to 10
House	4 x 4	enclosed	6 to 15

a box of mill-ends, short, uneven pieces of wood that most people burn. I knew something interesting could be made and arranged a dozen or so as a mosaic. A neighbor cuts similar shapes from plywood and arranges them in unusual patterns. Painted, they resemble plaster bas-reliefs. Panels such as these are effective on fences, walls, and gates.

Technical skills are seldom required. Consider wood sculptures, handsome columns that can be made without expertise. Use 4 x 4 or 6 x 6 timber for small ones, and logs or bridge timber for large ones. Make shallow cuts from different angles, then chisel the wood between the cuts until you create a pleasing design. For variety drill some holes. Tone with stain or paint or give the wood a "Japanese burned finish" with a butane torch. Columns can also be decorated with nails and other objects. Professional artists get hundreds of dollars for such columns.

With little more skill you can make cast plaster and concrete panels. The first one I made took less than an hour, cost less than five dollars, and was attractive enough to hang in our patio. You can duplicate my efforts with 30-mesh sand, plaster of Paris, and a sheet of expanded metal for backing.

Build a 2 x 4 frame (mine was 16 x 32 inches), tacking the corners lightly so the wood can be parted when the plaster hardens. Fill the frame half-full with sand, moistening lightly as you pour. Don't overwater; excess moisture makes the sand difficult to shape. The sand itself can be flat or contoured, depending on your design. Press various objects into it until you create an interesting design. For mine I used handles from discarded plumbing fixtures.

Casting plaster sets up quickly and you must work fast. Mix the plaster to the consistency of cream in small amounts to prevent hardening. Pour into the mold and repeat until the sand is covered with ½ inch of mix. Let it harden slightly, then place the metal backing. Cover with another ½ inch of plaster and let the panel harden. If the outer edges of backing are bent at right angles and allowed to protrude, they will create an edge for mounting.

After the plaster hardens, separate the frame and lift the cast. Some sand will cling to the face, but don't brush it off at this point. Most of it will fall free as it dries, in about twenty-four hours. What remains imbedded in the plaster enhances the sand-cast effect.

Other materials can be used for molding. Styrofoam is a plastic material with advantages. The tip of a heated soldering iron cuts through easily, and pattern-making is fast. Since the material is not as fragile to work with as sand, intricate edges can be well defined. Be sure to coat the surface with shortening, grease, or petroleum jelly before casting to ensure an easy release.

Panels can be displayed painted or unpainted. In either form they are not waterproof and should not be hung in unprotected areas. Shellac and plastic sprays give some protection, but when weatherproof plaques are required, use concrete. To reduce the weight of concrete, I combine vermiculite, sand, and Portland cement in a 3-2-2 mixture.

Small castings can be hung with wire, as you would a picture. Large ones need the support of wood or metal clips. These can be fastened to solid walls with bolts or long screws, but on thinner materials, such as plywood or gypsum, special fasteners will be required.

Split-wing toggle bolts and expansion screws are best, and both can fit predrilled holes. The inside section expands to increase the holding power. Either fastener can support 100 pounds.

Water as Garden Decoration

The early Chinese, Persians, and Egyptians made magnificent water gardens. Renaissance Italians used water with marvelous skill and exuberance in reflecting pools and fountains and cascades in city squares and superb private villas. The Villa d'Este at Tivoli is a vast hillside of rushing and leaping water. The Japanese considered water an essential component of garden design, and where there was none, implied it with patterns of stones.

Water can create an illusion as readily as it establishes a mood. I remember a rock wall beside an Arizona ranch house. The desert stood hot, dry, and forbidding, and the garden repeated this harshness with cactus and sage, yet a pipe near the top of the wall sent a trickle of water across the face of a few rocks to a small pond below, and its glistening wetness turned the place into an oasis.

Water can be used as effectively when still as when in motion. At rest, a shallow pool is a mirror reflecting the surroundings. In motion, it produces joyous, comforting sounds. Today, with an electric pump, you can add motion with little trouble and when you desire. Fountains and pools can be as active or as serene as you like. If you are lucky enough to have a natural stream, exploit its possibilities to the full.

Portable pools

Portable garden pools can be set above or below ground, and these are least expensive and easiest to install. They do not require changes in landscaping as excavated pools may do. Readymade designs in metal, concrete, and plastic are available from garden shops. Some have built-in fountains that connect to a hose or pump. Others are simple basins that must be filled by hand. Either type can be painted or decorated with mosaics to reflect color through the shimmer of water, and can be filled with rocks, plants, or fish. Iron basins acquire a mellow look when allowed to rust.

There are several ways to make portable pools. The easiest is with a discarded barbecue pan. When the legs are removed, the pan can be buried to the rim and filled with water. The hole for the grille post can be sealed with a metal patch or left to house a fountain nozzle.

A more complex pool can be made of plastic and wood. A friend in Denver built one for his deck using a 6 x 2 x 12-inch rough-wood frame and a 3 x 5-foot plastic pan. The ready-made pan was fastened inside the frame and a sufficient distance above the deck to accommodate a small 1/55-hp circulating pump below. Holes were cut in the pan for the pump intake and discharge. Since the fountain weighed less than 30 pounds empty, it could easily be drained and refilled.

Permanent pools

Large pools can be built in the ground. In swampy areas you may need no more than a natural depression or hollowed-out place in the earth, but where soil is porous, as in most regions, pools must be lined to hold water. Gunite, asphalt, concrete, or even building paper can be used, and large preformed containers, such as bathtubs, can be buried. The container is not important when the rim is below ground level. Plantings can hide the outline and the result treated as a natural pool.

Position is important. A pool close to a house, in the center of a garden, or uncomfortably near a path makes a garden seem small and cluttered. A pool away from traffic and out of the center of things seems to increase the size of a garden.

The easiest way to make a pool is to excavate the shape and depth desired, then line the hollow with concrete. With a rented concrete mixer, you can build a fair-sized pool in less than a day. If you dig the hole with care and keep the outline simple, it is not necessary to use forms to control the cement.

Pour the mix upon the ground, shaping the final surface as you pour. Be sure to tamp the earth to provide a solid base, and in colder areas spread a 3- to 5-inch layer of sand and gravel beneath the cement as a cushion against freezing. Use a rich mixture—4 parts sand and gravel to 1 part concrete—and a stiff one, with less than normal water, so the cement will hold its shape on the slopes. Pour the cement 4 to 6 inches thick, and for reinforcement, submerge chicken wire in the wet mix. For irregular shapes or a well-defined edge, use wooden or metal forms. (Concrete work is covered in more detail in Chapter 5.)

Be sure to include practical drainage arrangements. A pool must be emptied from time to time for cleaning, maintenance, and repair. The simplest system involves a drain installed when the pool is built. The drain is cemented into the bottom and a standard plumbing line connected to the sewer, or the drain can empty into a sump or the

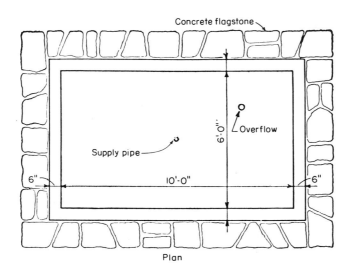

Concrete flagstone

Overflow

Supply pipe

6'-0"

6" 10'-0" 6"

Plan

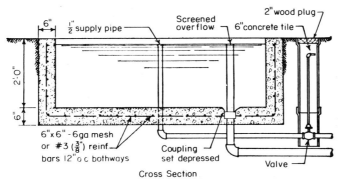

6" ½ supply pipe   Screened over flow   6" concrete tile   2" wood plug

2'-0"

6"

6"x6"-6ga mesh or #3 (⅜") reinf bars 12"o c bothways   Coupling set depressed   Valve

Cross Section
RECTANGULAR POOL

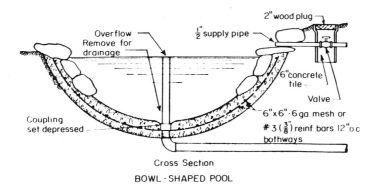

Overflow Remove for drainage   ½ supply pipe   2" wood plug

6" concrete tile

Valve

Coupling set depressed   6"x6"-6ga mesh or #3 (⅜") reinf bars 12"o c bothways

Cross Section
BOWL-SHAPED POOL

SMALL POOLS
A rectangular pool in plan and cross section; and (below) a circular pool for water plants, shown in cross section. The overflow pipe can be removed for drainage.
(Courtesy of Portland Cement Association)

garden. The line can be opened and closed with a submerged draincock or controlled by a remote handle, but a simpler method is the standpipe, a length of pipe screwed into the drain. The pipe stands upright and its height controls the depth of the pool. When the water rises above the standpipe it pours over the pipe rim and is drained away. The pool is emptied by removing the pipe.

Large pools are generally drained and cleaned on schedule, biweekly or monthly, depending on size and climate. Dirt and algae must be removed to prevent a troublesome build-up. However, you can reduce the need for cleaning in single-level pools by attaching a simple filter to a circulating system.

Place a submersible pump at the lowest point in the pool and add an intake line that reaches some distance from the pump. Place ½ to 1 inch of aquarium gravel beneath pump and intake lines, then cover with a screen and more aquarium gravel, up to 2½ inches if possible. Algae and dirt will be trapped in the gravel and screen as water is drawn into the pump, and bacteria in the water will consume the algae. The clear water is recirculated in a normal way through a line from pump to fountain nozzle. With this system a pool usually needs cleaning only twice a year. To facilitate maintenance, fit a rim of smooth tile at water level. The dirt ring, normal in any pool, can be wiped away with a sponge.

Fountains, bubblers, waterfalls

When pressurized water is important for one of these, you can draw it direct from the house piping, but in the interest of economy and conservation, consider a circulating pump. One filling works over and over again as naturally as a continuous fresh supply. Two types of circulating pumps can do the work, submersible and conventional. A submersible pump is, of course, made to rest in the water. No extra plumbing is required, except for the nozzle, and, in some cases, an extra line to replenish the water lost through evaporation. A conventional pump is mounted away from water, protected against the elements, with plumbing lines to draw water from one part of the pool and return it to another. Submersible pumps are excellent for single-level pools. Conventional pumps are satisfactory for multilayered types and waterfalls.

Attractive house numbers indicate more than your address. Here, readymade wooden numbers will be glued to a sheet of translucent plastic in handmade frame. Be sure to use waterproof glue.

The same, installed.

At night, with a light behind the plastic, the sign is a sure beacon for guests. L-v lighting is a good choice for this.

Nail metal numbers to separate lengths of 2 x 4, then place in the ground where they can be seen from a car.

On this rugged mailbox, post and crossbeam have been chipped with a hand ax to simulate an adz effect. Shingles repeat the roof design of the house.

Harmonizing with the raised planters beyond, a concrete-block column supports a custom-built metal box large enough for packages. Blocks are set on a footing of poured concrete.

A conventional box is camouflaged within a rectangular wooden shell. Compartment below is for packages. Concrete blocks echo the design of the wall.

Mailbox combined with a circular planter. Long slats look like shingles but with more uniform pattern. Brick is repeated as edging for walk and in wall (not shown).

A large stone was chiseled out near the top and pre-cast numbers glued in place. A deeper aperture was made for the standard readymade box.

Mailbox, repeating Oriental motif of house. The box is mounted on bamboo poles set in concrete. The translucent plastic backing against cut-out wooden sides gives a Shoji-screen effect. Garden of Mr. and Mrs. G. W. Harrington

Waterproof mailbox housed in a fanciful metal shell, the heavy feeling of metal negated by the openwork design.

Utilitarian weatherproof boxes made of wood, painted, and placed on 6 x 6 uprights set in concrete, hold a quantity of mail. Lid lifts for the mailman, and overlap edging provides the weather seal. Courtesy of Mr. and Mrs. George Mangan

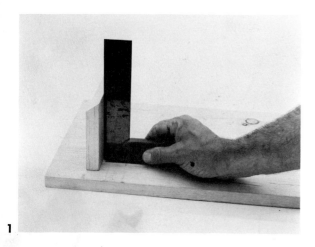

1

3

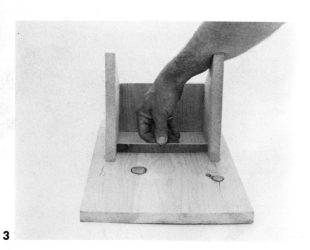

5

BIRD FEEDER:

Start with 1 x 12 lumber. Base and top are 18 inches long. Back is 4 inches high, sides are tapered from 4 in the rear to 8 in the front. (1) Attach the back piece to the base with galvanized nails from the bottom. Be sure it is square. (2) Attach side pieces to the base and back piece with nails. (3) Insert a lip in the front to keep grain or feed from spilling. If you saw a shallow groove in the side pieces, plywood lip can be inserted easily. (4) Nail top to sides and back. (5) Add a front perch. Then mount in the yard. I've mounted mine on a 1-inch pipe secured to the bottom with a standard flange mounting.

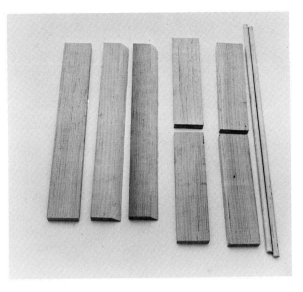

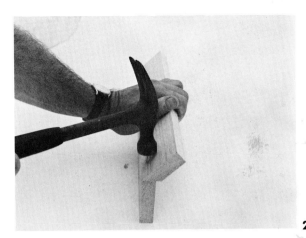

2

3

4

OPEN FEEDER:

(1) Pieces required: One bottom board 1 x 4 inches to 14 inches long. Two side boards the same, but one edge of each tapered at 45°. Four end pieces 6 inches long. Two ½-inch dowels 18 inches long. (2) Attach one angled board to the bottom with galvanized finishing nails. Attach second angled board the same way. (3) Add end pieces. Be sure edges are spaced equally. (4) Drill ½-inch holes in end pieces. (These could be drilled before assembling but are shown in this sequence to make construction clearer.) (5) Insert ½-inch dowel on both sides. Add second end pieces (also drilled) for decoration. (6) Attach chain or wires to eye screws and hang the feeder. Fill with seed or grain and await customers.

5

6

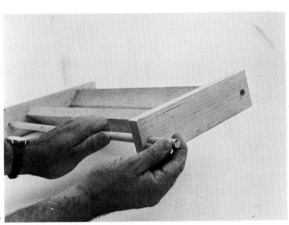

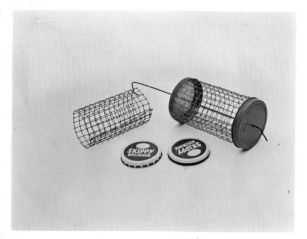

A practically squirrelproof hanging bird feeder for suet is made from two jar tops and a section of chicken wire bent to fit. A straightened-out wire coat hanger, the ends hooked, holds things together, and for good looks the jar tops are painted.

Natural house for woodpecker made from a hollowed section of tree (in this case alder). Cut and remove an L-shaped section from the base, then chisel or drill a nesting area inside the remaining part. Drill a hole of 1½-inch diameter in the L-piece and nail or screw it to the original position. A dowel makes perching easier and may also attract other species of bird.

Rustic type of birdhouse is mostly for woodpeckers, but occasionally used by wrens, chickadees, and others.

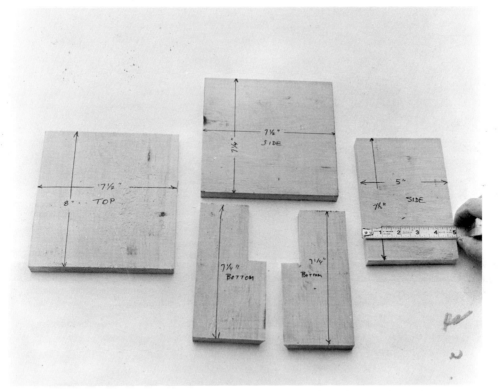

Open-platform birdhouse shown in sections. Use 1-inch boards or plywood. Measurements are for medium-sized structure. Assemble with nails or nails and glue.

Enclosed house, which appeals to a greater number of birds. Dimensions are for a basic design developed by Dick Irwin, of Kentucky. This is considered standard and has been used by Scouts, 4-H Clubs, and others in many states. Bottom piece has two corners cut for drainage. Front is hinged for cleaning.

Some religious objects, shrines particularly, seem appropriate in certain gardens. This figure in a simple shelter is handled sincerely. Marc Askew, designer

Timbers make excellent decorations. This post has been sculptured with a saw, then ornamented with nails. A stimulating suggestion of what imagination can achieve most simply.

Sawed and chiseled posts make unusual garden ornaments. Essential tools are a saw (electric, hand, table, or radial) and a couple of chisels. Ceramic and wooden objects may be attached. Nut Tree Restaurant, Nut Tree, California. Bob McCabe, artist

Patio doors and fences can be accented with small carved pieces. Carving soft woods is easy; patterns can be traced from magazines and books. Four or five tools will suffice: a flat chisel, two gouges, and two V-groove cutters. Marc Askew, designer

Elegant fence designs are made from inexpensive objects. These copper plaques, tacked together in a redwood frame, add interest to an otherwise monotonous pattern.

A frame relieves the starkness of this wall in an entry. It was made from thin wood slats and amber plastic. The shadows it casts also give an illusion of depth. Lloyd Bond, L.A.

Simple objects may make unusual decorations. Cast-iron trivets can simply be hung (they are handsome enough), but we decided to frame ours in heavy redwood for a silhouette against the sky.

Sand-casting is easy and can be used for plaster or concrete panels. Use a fine-mesh sand; this is 30-mesh. Pour a 3 x 4 frame half full, then moisten gently. Excess moisture makes sand difficult to work.

Sand can be leveled or contoured, depending on the desired final design. We chose to make variations on the surface of the mold. Kitchen utensils can be used for scooping.

Design can be made by drawing or by pressing objects into the sand. Since I have little drawing ability, I used discarded plumbing handles as stampers. The depressions become raised designs on the finished panel. Almost anything that makes an impression can be used. Try for a variation in sizes.

Plaster is mixed to the consistency of light cream and poured over the mold. Pour a ½-inch layer, then add expanded metal backing, and pour another ½-inch of plaster. Expanded metal has been allowed to protrude at ends. These ears will be used for hanging when the panel dries.

Finished panel, lifted from the mold. It can be hung framed or unframed, in its natural color or painted. Plaster should not be hung in an unprotected area. When weatherproof panels are needed, use concrete.

Clay decorations strung on leather and hung from a patio tree. Clay must be fired for all-weather use. Marc Askew, designer

Clay tiles before firing. Designs are made with circle cutters or other utensils, or are hand-drawn. The ability to draw representational objects is not needed, and hardly appropriate. Marc Askew, designer

The finished tiles screwed to the top of a fence.

A large clay panel sounds the keynote in a back garden. Composed of non-realistic forms; this is a kind of ornament that anyone with imagination and a sense of design could create. Marc Askew, designer

Close-up of part of the panel (above right) before firing. Design elements are surprisingly simple.

Variation in color, texture, and dark to light, here achieved with stones, wood, and foliage. U.C.L.A.

Stones can suggest water where there is none. A simple pattern of river-smoothed rocks between banks of green leads the eye as it would follow a flowing stream. Garden of Mrs. Gretchen Plechner

A little water goes a long way. The trickle from the lion's mouth and the small splash on the brick patio gives an illusion of far greater wetness. Eriksson, Peters & Thoms, L.A.

In Japan, stone basins stand outside teahouses. Participants in the tea ceremony wash their hands, at the same time symbolically washing away the noisy outside world. The inscription identifies the stone as a "dew catcher." Dipper is bamboo. U.C.L.A.

An artificial pool is given a natural look with an edging of stones set in concrete. Plants are grown in submerged containers and arranged carefully as part of the design. U.C.L.A.

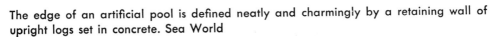

The edge of an artificial pool is defined neatly and charmingly by a retaining wall of upright logs set in concrete. Sea World

A shallow basin gives an impression of more water and creates a mood of serenity. Similar pools can be made from discarded barbecue pans. Part of the effect of water is determined by the container. Water at rest expresses balance and stability. Garrett Eckbo, L.A.

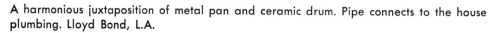

A harmonious juxtaposition of metal pan and ceramic drum. Pipe connects to the house plumbing. Lloyd Bond, L.A.

A sophisticated and architectural pool. One section is shallow for display, the other deeper for swimming. Combined, the unexpected expanse of water is impressive. Garden of Mr. and Mrs. Arthur Shapiro. Jocelyn Domela, L.A.

Another part of the same pool. With rhythm and restraint, rocks and plants are brought together inside and outside the pool. Bridge leads over water to continue walks.

The formal basins are reminiscent of Italian gardens, but the planting and stones have a Japanese feeling.

Three nozzles send water at different speeds and heights across clay pots and can be adjusted to work in unison or in sequence. Plumbing shops can help with the selection of similar pre-assembled fixtures. A salient part of the character of water is the rate of its flow. Marc Askew, designer

Plantings can be interesting in a pool when confined, as are these simple groups of reeds in handmade ceramic pots. Lytton Center, Oakland

The welcome presence of water is ingeniously provided here. A ring of pipe sends up a shower that takes away the curse of a scorching day. Bed of gravel for quick absorption. Braemar Homes, Los Angeles. Armstrong and Sharfman, L.A.

3

Outdoor Lighting

Contrary to a popular preconception, outdoor lighting is rarely a luxury or extravagance. The right combination of fixtures more than pays its way by adding a usable dimension to the hours of darkness. Lighting can make a garden a round-the-clock place. It can also add a sense of drama or mystery to plants and decorations. In short, the right system is a sensible investment in safety, security, utility, and beauty.

Gas fixtures, generally more decorative than utilitarian, are installed by professionals, but electrical systems, decorative *and* utilitarian, can be installed without special training. Recent developments offer a choice of two systems: conventional 120-volt lighting and the new l-v (low-voltage) lighting. Both have distinct advantages.

120-volt lighting

This long-established system gives brilliant illumination and offers a wider selection of fixtures. It is found in most older gardens that are lighted, and its reliability is unquestioned. But, on the debit side, the relatively high voltage is dangerous, complicated to install, and costly to operate.

Installation requires a city or county permit. You should check with the Building Department of your town both for regulations and for approved materials and equipment. Requirements vary across the country, and are especially flexible in the field of underground wiring. Some areas accept direct-burial cable. Others approve only the more costly metal conduit.

Don't stint on wire. Use heavier gauges for a full margin of safety. Insist on 12- or 14-gauge for lines to 100 feet and loads to 1,450 or 1,500 watts. Use 10- or 12-gauge for longer lines and loads to 1,950 or 2,000 watts. Bury the wire deep to protect against accidental damage.

In areas under cultivation, attach the wire to a board and bury the wood above the line. Don't cover the underground work until it has been checked by an inspector. Where lines rise above ground, use metal conduit for strength and extra protection. Be sure to use waterproof outlets and switches.

L-v lighting

This is low voltage, not low level, although the effect is underplayed when compared with the glare of 120-volt lighting. The l-v lighting uses a lower current, 12 volts, like that in your car, and is completely safe. Even direct contact cannot harm a child. Installations are so simple that a weekend gardener can create a fairly extensive system without problems and without city or county permit. (A complex installation may require a permit.) Fixtures are small, lightweight, and easily hidden. Several can be operated in unison for pennies a week. The selection of fixtures is limited, and the number that can be used on any circuit is restricted, but despite these drawbacks l-v lighting is ideal for the do-it-yourself gardener. I installed and used the Corolite system, and it has given trouble-free operation. The manufacturer (Corolite, a division of Coronado Manufacturing Company, 1205 East Hill Street, Long Beach, California 90806) offers a catalog and a page of hints for easier installation.

The transformer

The heart of an l-v system is the transformer that reduces 120 volts to 12 volts. It plugs into any outlet without complicated connections. It is available in sizes from 72 to 300 watts. The transformer size controls the number of fixtures and the length of wire that can be used. A 72-watt model is limited to three or four lights and 100 feet of wire. A 300-watt model can normally handle two 100-foot lengths of wire and six to eight lights. The smaller transformer costs thirty dollars, and the larger less than fifty dollars. When you compare initial expense and future utility, it makes sense to order a larger transformer even when you do not immediately need its capacity. A 126-watt type is considered adequate for the average installation.

The simplest transformer mounting is beside an outlet; the ideal mounting is directly to its own line. Either way, performance is best when the main lines—those carrying 12 volts from transformer to fixtures—are short. Some voltage is absorbed by the wires, and shorter lines reduce the loss measurably. It is better to use two short lines than one longer one, but short lines are often possible only when the transformer is mounted a substantial distance from the 120-volt outlet. This installation is preferred because a remote transformer mounting has its own lead-in and because the length of wire between the 120-volt outlet and transformer has no effect on the 12-volt operation. Most transformers are weatherproof when installed as directed by the manufacturer.

Switches and timers

A 12-volt system can be controlled by plugs, switches, or automatic timers. The simplest method is to plug and unplug the transformer, but switches and timers are obviously better. Switches can be inserted in the 120-volt line before the transformer, or in the l-v line after it. A switch after the transformer will need a relay and doorbell wiring. If you are not familiar with the basic mechanics of either approach, let a professional electrician install the controls while you do the rest of the work.

If you prefer a switchless system, use automatic controls. Many transformers have built-in timers that can be set to turn lights on and off at the hours you choose. The newest can be programmed for a full year, adjusting the hours that lights are switched on and off to coincide with daily changes in sunset and sunrise. Photoelectric cells do a similar job, but instead of reacting to time, they react to light.

The 12-volt main lines resemble appliance cord with a heavier weatherproof covering. They should be buried below the depth of normal garden cultivation, at least 6 inches. Bury the lines beside walks, planters, and pipelines to reduce the danger of accidental cutting. Where lines cross a lawn, use a flat shovel, push the blade deep, part the grass, and drop the wire behind it. Close the opening and push the edges of grass together. It will soon cover the scar.

Fixtures

Fixtures include sealed-beam and open-filament bulbs in spot, mushroom, and flood types. Some concentrate light, others flood it. Try each at night before you decide on final placement. Not even a professional can be certain of effects until he sees the lights in action. Try various fixtures in different positions. A change in the quantity or quality of light or in the angle makes a remarkable difference in the effect.

Most fixtures can be connected directly to the main line (some snap over the cable) or to stub-feeders, short extensions between the main line and fixture. Stub-lines are generally preferred because they allow a more direct main line, reducing its length and voltage loss. Note: Manufacturers of 12-volt systems recommend 12-gauge wire for lines no longer than 100 feet, but greater distance can often be gained with an increase in gauge size when no alternative is available. The larger the wire, the less the voltage drop. I use 12-gauge wire to 100 feet, 10-gauge to 200 feet, and 8-gauge to 300 feet. In every case stub-lines should be of 14- or 16-gauge.

Wires can be joined with solder, or by screw-on or crimped connectors. The last two are used by professionals and are recommended. Be sure to cover unions with a rubber compound or waterproof friction tape to prevent corrosion from fertilizer. When installing lights in planted areas, leave a foot of loose wire beside each fixture to allow for adjustment as plantings grow.

Colors are created by filters that snap or screw to the fixture. Six or seven hues are generally available, from blue through amber and pink. Use them sparingly. Colored lights should be accents only. Too many make a garden unreal and garish. Some people like to include a dimmer switch in the system, a control that regulates the level of illumination. The controls are reliable on 120-volt circuits, but the ones I've seen are hard on transformers, increasing wear, and are not recommended.

Candlelight

Electric lights are basic in any garden, but the final touch, surprisingly, is supplied most effectively by a more primitive source—candles. The spell of candlelight adds excitement to a party, and the holders can be as important as the candles themselves. Striking bases can be made from commonplace objects.

Try the clear-glass chimneys from camping lanterns. Use them singly on fences and in groups on patios. Clusters with bright candles look authentically Spanish. Glass jars give a similar effect. Metal castings and ceramic containers are easily adapted. Construction tile can be used. I rely on T-end drain tile. With 4 x 4 blocks inside to elevate the candles, the sparkling light is joyous.

Flare pots are especially attractive beside pools and on patios. I make them from coffee cans by punching a hole in the top and adding a wick and enough kerosene to give an hour of flame.

The possibilities range far beyond the conventional candle-in-a-wide-bottle, but you can discover them only when you take time to experiment.

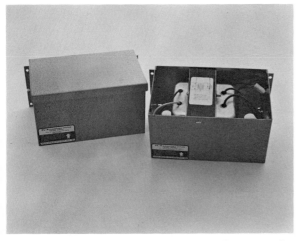

You can choose either 120-volt or 12-volt systems for garden lights; 12-volt is recommended because it is safe and simple to assemble. The heart of the system is a transformer, available in sizes from 75 to 300 watts (model shown is the largest).

Low-voltage wiring can be connected by screw-on clips, special connectors, or solder. The special connectors shown do not require stripping, i.e., removal of the insulation.

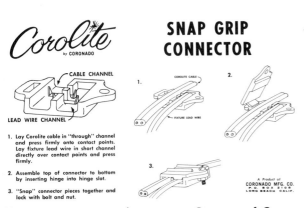

Corolite by CORONADO

SNAP GRIP CONNECTOR

CABLE CHANNEL

LEAD WIRE CHANNEL

1. Lay Corolite cable in "through" channel and press firmly onto contact points. Lay fixture lead wire in short channel directly over contact points and press firmly.

2. Assemble top of connector to bottom by inserting hinge into hinge slot.

3. "Snap" connector pieces together and lock with bolt and nut.

A Product of
CORONADO MFG. CO.
P. O. BOX 2108
LONG BEACH CALIF.

How to use a patented connector. Courtesy of Coronado Mfg. Co.

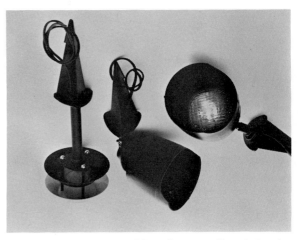

Low-voltage fixtures, although not offered in the variety of 120-volt types, come in several designs and heights. Some, as on left, concentrate the light. Others, on right, yield a broader beam. Casings of dark-colored plastics make them inconspicuous.

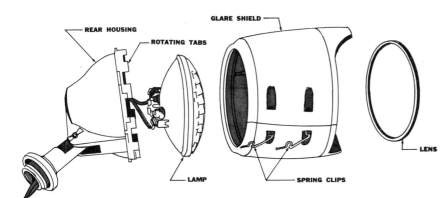

REAR HOUSING

ROTATING TABS

GLARE SHIELD

LAMP

SPRING CLIPS

LENS

A 12-volt light disassembled to show parts. Lenses and lamps can be changed quickly. Instructions are supplied. Lenses need be changed only to change color. Courtesy of Coronado Mfg. Co.

An abruptly curving path is illuminated by a bell light, set high to throw a relatively broad beam. A lower light focused on the background increases the illusion of depth. Garden of Mr. and Mrs. Harold Hecht. Jocelyn Domela, L.A.

A mushroom light is mounted on one side of a rock by a pool. It illumines portions of the rock, curb, and water. Garden of Mr. and Mrs. Arthur Shapiro. Jocelyn Domela, L.A.

Gas is becoming popular for garden lighting. This lantern, adapted from an antique, is mounted on a patio wall. Residence of Mr. and Mrs. Harold Hecht. Jocelyn Domela, L.A.

Stone lanterns can be used for electricity, gas, or candles. Reproductions of old lanterns are available from garden centers.

Light post assembled from wood and plastic. The clear-plastic shield softens light.

CONSTRUCTING TWO LIGHT POSTS FOR AN ENTRANCE

(1) (Left) Shell is made from 1 x 6 redwood with 2 x 4 uprights. Corners are mitered, and uprights are inset for perfect fit.

(2) (Right) Uprights are decorated with heavy dowels set into drilled holes. Dowels are secured with waterproof glue. Since the fixture will be painted, they are not of matching wood but of hardwood.

(3) (Left) Assembled frame shows how the 1 x 6 collar and uprights are fitted.

(4) (Right) A decorative crown is made to fit on top. Octagonal shape is contrived from 2 x 4s with the ends tapered and inset.

(5) (Left) Watertight top is made from 2 x 6 redwood. To cut unit pieces of the octagon, the blade of a power saw is set at 22.5°. Sections should be fastened with waterproof glue and finishing nails.

(6) (Right) Completed light posts, decorated with tile, are modern and dramatic. Frosted plastic center softens the light. Marc Askew, designer

Garden lighting is often a necessity. Here one light on a short standard reveals the edge of a pool. Judicious planting adds to the harmony. Marc Askew, designer

Lights can combine modern and period styles. This one has an early-English heritage. The panes are unbreakable textured and colored plastic. Brass fasteners came from a furniture supply store. Marc Askew, designer

Candleholders can be made from discards. (Below) A cracked glass shade, originally a wall-mount for an electric light in the 1930s, was inverted to hide the broken lip, set in a wooden base, and routed to accept the lip. It makes a handsome, modern holder.

1

Garden lights can be made from junk parts. (1) This World War II bomb rack is available as surplus along the West Coast for less than three dollars. (2) We made a wooden base and added flush-mounted light sockets and two bolts to hold the rack. Since the light is placed under the eaves, sockets need not be water-proof. (3) Wall-mounted with 25-watt bulbs inside, the light is connected to a switch on the wall and coupled to other outdoor lights. One switch turns everything on.

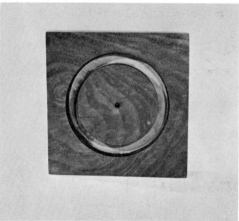

2

3

4

Benches, Seats, and Tables

Gardens and patios enable us to enjoy relaxing out-of-doors and should be thoughtfully furnished with the right combination of chairs, lounges, benches, and tables. Not many gardens are comfortably furnished, in good part because well-designed ready-made equipment is expensive and not always available. Even when good, it may not have the styling to harmonize with your own garden and may look out of place or much too conspicuous. On the other hand, nothing can accord so well with your garden, and save space, as built-in seats and other equipment and custom-made portable pieces. You can get great satisfaction by combining ready-made articles with some that you have designed and made.

Portable Furniture

Portable furniture has the obvious advantage of mobility. It can be moved to follow the sun or shade, the change of seasons, arranged to promote sociability or privacy, and stored to assure maximum life.

Ready-made plans

Prepared plans include drawings, dimensions, instructions, and a list of materials. Standards, such as plans for redwood chairs and lounges, can be purchased for less than a dollar from local sources and are often also available from the California Redwood Association (617 Montgomery Street, San Francisco, California 94100). Designs for plywood pieces are sometimes featured in home, garden, and handyman magazines. A wide range of plans can be purchased from the American Plywood Association (Tacoma, Washington 98400). Ideas for similar projects in composition hardboards are available from several manufacturers. Georgia-Pacific Corporation (Commonwealth Building, Portland, Oregon 92707) and Masonite Corporation (Dover, Ohio 44622) are two.

If good design is desirable, utility is essential, and when furniture can do more than one job, it saves space and money. Chairs with wide arms avoid the need for side tables. Extra-wide benches can be used for seating and sunbathing, and smaller ones can double as coffee tables. Many recent designs have been conceived with this adaptability in mind and are sturdy enough to use the year round where climate permits.

Measurements

A piece of movable furniture should not weigh more than 35 pounds unless fitted with casters or made to knock apart. The maximum seat height is 19 inches (by comparison a dining chair is 16 or 17 inches). When canted, i.e. higher in front than rear, it can be 5 or 6 inches lower. Lounge chairs can be as low as 6 inches with a correspondingly deeper seat. A 15-inch-square seat bottom is minimal and one 15 deep by 19 wide is better. Allow at least 22 inches width per person when building benches and 26 if the bench doubles as a table. Tables have three usable heights: 18 inches—coffee table; 19 inches—serving table doubling as a bench; 28½ inches—standard dining height.

Whether you build from prepared or original plans, understand the full construction sequence before you begin. Know how each part will be joined. If furniture-building is new to you, begin with a simple plywood stool (see photo). You can cut one by hand in minutes from a 2-foot square of ¾-inch plywood. A standard 4 x 8-foot sheet will make eight stools for less than ten dollars.

Tables

Tables can be made of various materials. Use redwood to make a cross-legged picnic type. Use fir and plywood to build a side table as you might an oversized stool. If you are lucky enough to discover a discarded wooden core from a roll of wire cable, you have the start of a unique pedestal design. Sand the wood to remove splinters and lettering, then protect with spar varnish or paint.

Drainage and flue tiles and concrete stepping rounds offer possibilities. On a patio, set the tiles upright as they are or weighted with concrete, and top with wood or concrete rounds. In a garden, bury one end for stability, then fill with sand to the final 1 to 2 inches. Spread latex patching cement around and inside the rim, then set a concrete round in place.

Portability means storage; storage means space. In warm climates temporary space may be all you need, perhaps an area beneath the overhang of a building, but in less temperate climates an enclosed shelter is required. Storage can be fitted into spare corners of a garage or workroom if you have only a few articles. When you have more, a special building or room will be far more satisfactory. Assemble-them-yourself aluminum buildings make good storage places. When furniture knocks apart, spatial demands are slight, but when furniture is permanently assembled, space should be organized. Folding chairs can be hung on racks or stored upright or piled. Lounges can be placed against walls or flat on the floor. Tables can be turned end-to-end.

Built-in Furniture

Built-in furniture minimizes clutter, obviates the storage problem, and helps to define or accentuate a garden area. Most types are easily built. A hammer-and-saw man can assemble a piece as quickly as a person with a complete workshop.

Benches

Benches are a popular project. One reason for this was expressed by a landscape architect in Minneapolis when he said: "I build them where they can be seen all winter. The sight of a bench gives warmth to the coldest day." Benches do extend a year-round invitation to share a favorite view or private place. Good benches are also useful near fire pits and in work areas. They are most welcome in a place of cool shade. You will generally arrange seating so that people face away from afternoon sun, but you can put one bench in shade and another in sun to give guests a choice. Benches longer than 8 or 10 feet should be curved, or halved at a right angle to form conversation centers. People usually avoid long, straight seats and cluster at one end.

The secret of good bench-building lies in the supports. End pieces should be sturdy and in scale. Metal, wood, concrete, and brick are possibilities. A popular and easy-to-build bench support is made of a short length of 1½- or 2-inch galvanized pipe. With one end buried in concrete, the pipe is capable of holding heavy loads. A narrow bench needs one pipe length at each end; a wider one may require two lengths.

Practical end pieces can be made from 2 x 12s, especially when

buried in concrete. Use them as you would pipe, in 2-foot sections with
1 foot below grade and set in 9 inches of concrete. If wood is exposed,
cover the buried end with a preservative. Wooden supports can also be
anchored to metal stirrups set in concrete. Choose the stirrup sized for
the lumber you use. The California Redwood Association recommends
hot-dipped galvanized iron or aluminum with redwood.

For variation, try clay tile. Weighted with concrete, tile has the
strength and stability to become an excellent support. I prefer oval flue
tiles. I fill them with concrete with two foundation bolts per flue. When
the concrete hardens, I bolt 2 x 4s across each, then place the bench
tops. If benches are straight, tops can be made from various lumbers,
from 1 x 4 to 2 x 12 pieces. For curved benches, thinner materials
shape better. Choose 2 x 2 or 1 x 4 (on end) when the wood follows
a curve. Thicker woods can be used only in short sections across the
bench.

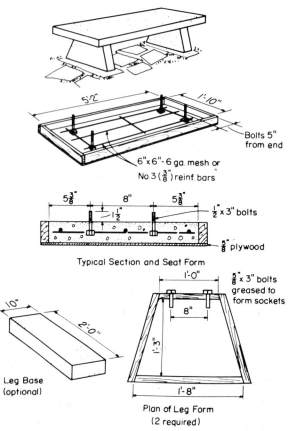

Typical Section and Seat Form

Leg Base
(optional)

Plan of Leg Form
(2 required)

LAWN BENCH

**GARDEN BENCH CAST
IN CONCRETE**
**Two upper drawings show
the seat section, which is
reinforced with ½-inch rod.
Lower right, the plan for
the leg form. A base for
the leg is also shown. It
can be used to level and
support the legs but it is
not required.**
(Courtesy of Portland Cement
Association)

Sun tables

Consider the versatility of the extra-wide bench, especially its new variation, the sun table—a structure too wide to be a proper bench, too low to be a true table. Children play on it, adults sun on it, families use it for snacks, picnics, displays, and hobbies. I've seen tables as wide as 12 feet, and many that are 8 or 10 feet. Square ones can be cut with hand tools, round ones shaped by saber or band saw. If you have neither tool, build a square bench and let a cabinet shop do the cutting. Oversized tables are especially handy beside swimming pools and patios, where they will find multiple use.

Cushions add comfort and color. For durability, be sure the core is plastic or foam rubber (plastic is less expensive); for comfort, insist on a 4- or 5-inch thickness. If you need several pads, cut your own from a sheet of foam. For straight lines, try sawing rather than cutting; for contours, you must use scissors.

Select coverings on the basis of durability, texture, and color. Many plastics are good because they *could* be left outside for the whole year—but they can get uncomfortably hot in direct sun. Sailcloth and canvas are excellent, but most require frequent airing and drying to prevent mildew. Many people like the colors and textures of these fabrics: soft, warm shades of yellow, orange, and pink, and cool tones of blue, navy, and black.

Materials and Techniques

Building garden furniture without technical skill may seem to be a tall order, but it is not, for two reasons: Garden pieces often have a rustic massiveness that allows an acceptable margin of error, and they can be made of softwoods, the easiest material to use. Redwood, cypress, and cedar are the most durable and I prefer them, but with new preservatives many other softwoods are safe outdoors. Exterior plywood is also good, although some professional designers tend to disagree. Fir plywood, for example, may check, but the checking can be controlled by painting.

Use first-quality lumber for all exposed parts. Lesser grades, with loose knots, can be used for parts not directly exposed to weather. Wood with flat grain will weather better if the bark side is out. You can distinguish the bark side by the growth rings: On flat-grained wood the rings curve toward the bark in the center and toward the heart at the edges.

Use 2-inch-thick boards or 1-inch plywood on conventionally framed tables and seats. Thinner materials will require more support. The wider the wood, the greater the chance of warping. With 10- or 12-inch lumber, allow ¼-inch clearance between pieces for expansion. When furniture can be stored, kiln-dried wood minimizes warping.

Assemble projects with nails, bolts, screws, glue, or a combination of these. Nails are satisfactory for light work, bolts insure rigidity on heavier pieces, and screws assure neatness with durability midway between the two. Glue increases the strength of all three and should be used when possible. To prevent staining, use rustproof nails, bolts, and screws, and for permanence, waterproof glue.

If you drill holes slightly smaller than the shank, wood screws will enter easier, with less chance of splitting. To hide screwheads and bolt-heads and to prevent snagging, countersink the holes. For the same effect with nails, use finishing nails and sink the heads with a nail set. Fill holes with a non-oily filler to prevent discoloration.

Power tools are not essential. Furniture was made, and obviously well made, long before they were invented. However, I would dislike working without at least three—an electric handsaw, a ¼- or ⅜-inch drill, and an orbital sander. This basic kit can increase the speed, accuracy, and neatness of your work. If you become interested in a more elaborate shop or in learning how to handle power tools, you might take a woodworking course at a local high school. Adult night courses are usually excellent, rates reasonable, and one term can make you proficient with many tools.

GARDEN STOOL:

(1) Easily built from one 2 x 2-foot section of ¾-inch plywood. Draw a square in the center of the board, arranged so triangular corners remain. (2) After cutting, you have one square section, the seat, and four triangular pieces for legs. Cut the corners from these pieces. The dimensions are optional (i.e., the leg height), but cut the four the same size. (3) Join the legs at one end in pairs. For strength back the joint with squares of 1 x 2 or 2 x 2. (4) Attach the legs to the seat. Be sure the legs are evenly spaced. Legs can be nailed, screwed, or glued. I used finishing nails. (5) Reinforce the legs from the top with additional finishing nails. Then sand the surface and finish with varnish, shellac, wax, or paint.

1

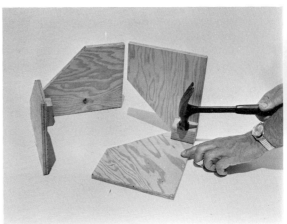

3

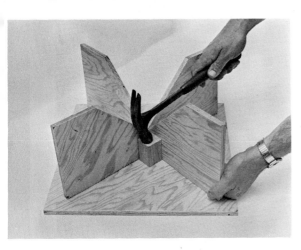

5

(Left) A built-in bench such as this should be planned before the patio pavement is poured so that the uprights and the light fixture can be placed permanently in the concrete. Marc Askew, designer. (Right) Uprights are 6 x 6 redwood timbers sunk into the ground, held in place with concrete. The patio floor is poured around them for a finished appearance and additional support. Supports are placed 4 to 6 feet apart, depending on the thickness of the bench planking. Ends can be cut to level after concrete has hardened.

A wide bench that tends to look heavy can be made to appear lighter with wood spaced apart. When thin boards are used, as 1 x 4s are here, they must be set on end for strength. The edging is 2 x 6, beveled. Uprights pass through the bench to support a roof.

A simple lounge in Spanish design, made of 6 x 6 and 1 x 6 lumber. Legs are decorated with a single line.

Side pieces are fitted to the legs, which have an inset or dado cut to fit. End pieces are further supported with L-brackets.

Side pieces are also secured to the legs with wood screws. Two are used on each end.

Screws are countersunk with heads hidden with plugs (cut from the same wood). Plugs are set into screw holes, then cut level with surface. They are held in place with waterproof glue. When the wood is finished, plugs will not show.

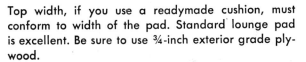

Top width, if you use a readymade cushion, must conform to width of the pad. Standard lounge pad is excellent. Be sure to use ¾-inch exterior grade plywood.

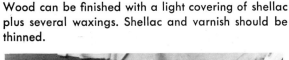

Wood can be finished with a light covering of shellac plus several waxings. Shellac and varnish should be thinned.

(Left) Seating can do double duty. This *engawa* is both a step and a small seat beside a bedroom garden; 2 x 2 material, carefully spaced, creates a pleasant transition. Marc Askew, designer. (Right) In the foreground, a seat serves as a barrier on the edge of the deck. Building code of many communities requires barrier at any open drop, and this type meets the legal requirements. In the distance is a platform with portable rattan seating. Garden of Mr. and Mrs. Arthur Shapiro. Jocelyn Domela, L.A.

Seat of 2 x 6 timber is set on end. Well-finished, painted black, the platform gains in design through its floating appearance. Lawrence Halprin and Associates, L.A.

Open seating built around a small garden pool repeats the protected seating in the gazebo, though 2 x 4 planking is used in one and wider lumber in the other. Marc Askew, designer

A round bench works handsomely around a tree. Sometimes such benches are combined with planters. Garden of Mr. and Mrs. Montgomery Fisher

This most effective simple design is well made of 4 x 6 end pieces and 2 x 8 planking and edging. Richard A. Campbell, A.I.A.

Metal supports are easy to use and reliable. Square tubing is modern and good-looking. Top is of 2 x 6 planking cut slightly narrow to reduce the visual weight. Foothill Square. Lawrence Halprin and Associates, L.A.

The simplest support is galvanized metal pipe set in the ground (and best in concrete) with the top flanged to accept the cross pieces. Top is of 1 x 6 boards. Strybing Arboretum

A low bench set off by an ornate, dominating light. Marc Askew, designer

A rustic bench made from discarded bridge timbers. The dark, weathering paint contributes to the design. Richard A. Campbell, A.I.A.

An interesting bench-top design: Four 4 x 8 planks form the top, but the ends are finished with a cross section of thinner material mitered for a neat appearance. Theodore Osmundson and Associates, L.A.

Benches with a length greater than 8 or 10 feet are rarely successful in one line. The bench becomes more useful when it is right-angled or curved.

The large and low sun table can be used for seating, sunbathing, dining, and children's play. Marc Askew, designer

A table assembled from a concrete round and a drain tile.

5

Walks, Paths, Steps, and Bridges

Walks are main highways built to carry people promptly from one point to another. Paths are secondary lanes, not concerned with the speed and wear of traffic. Together they greatly affect the functioning and appearance of a garden. When the layout, design, and materials are suited to the particular area and related to their surroundings, the result is unmistakably right and inconspicuous. The Japanese are most successful in this basic element of their sensitive landscape designs.

In the beginning

The choice of dimension, design, and material depends upon purpose. A *walk* should be wide and smooth for easy movement—and usually straight, since a straight line is the shortest, if least exciting, route. A *path* can be narrower, rougher, and less direct. Even a slight bend adds interest, and successive curves slow your pace and make you more aware of the surroundings. When it is difficult to decide on the contours, define the general route with a long garden hose, shaping it until the line seems right, then mark with stakes. Of course, avoid fussy turns unless for some specific reason; do not force the hose much beyond its inclination. Bear in mind the future look, particularly the height, of planting along the path.

A walk is only as reliable as its foundations are thorough. Layout, excavation, and subsurfacing must not be hurried. To determine the necessary excavation, drive stakes 2 to 3 feet apart the length of the walk. If it is a long one, divide the project into easy-to-handle 4- to 8-foot sections. Mark the elevation of the final surface on the first stake, then stretch a line the full length. Since the string represents the finished

71

surface it should be either parallel to the soil, following all variations in soil level, or entirely level itself if the walk is to be on one plane. The choice depends on the terrain.

The earth must be excavated sufficiently below the string to allow for the base plus the surface material, usually 6 to 8 inches. For example, base gravel is spread 2 to 4 inches deep, and concrete is then poured 3 to 4 inches above the base for walks, and 6 inches for driveways.

In a few well-drained, firm soils the base can be eliminated, but even there a bottom layer of gravel or clay soil increases durability. Usually 3 inches of medium gravel will minimize the damages of water and freezing. Excessive moisture should be carried off by drainage, a procedure outlined in Chapter 9.

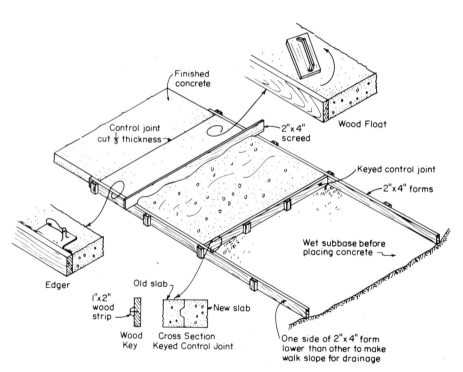

CONCRETE WALKS

Walks can be accurately poured between running forms of 2 x 4 and can be stopped at any point with a cross-dam of similar material. On long walks it is wise to pour in sections so that you can control all stages of pouring and surfacing the wet mix and can allow for expansion. Be sure to include a smooth joint between new and old sections as shown (keyed control joint).

(Courtesy of Portland Cement Association)

Concrete

Whenever a broad expanse of practical, reliable, all-weather paving is needed, concrete is the general choice. Its color and texture contrast agreeably with foliage and act as a foil. Some designers consider the look of concrete cold and impersonal, but the effect depends upon the surroundings and the proximity and density of relieving foliage. Also, concrete can be colored and given interesting textures and patterns. It is easy to mix, shape, and maintain.

Concrete is a combination of cement, gravel, and sand, hardened by the chemical reaction between cement and water. If you must pour a large area quickly, get professional help, but if the area is small or if you can divide a large one into sections, the operation is a quite feasible home project. The cement can be premixed or homemade. Amounts of a cubic yard or more can be ordered from Transit-Mix or Ready-Mix suppliers. Theoretically, premix costs only a little more than homemade (when you include materials, equipment rentals, and other factors), but there are no guarantees. Transit-Mix trucks will rarely deliver less than 1 cubic yard (100 square feet of 4-inch paving), and most firms add substantial penalties when a truck is not emptied quickly. A newer service, limited to large cities, offers smaller quantities of Ready-Mix in returnable dump trailers that you can tow behind your car.

For most home projects, cement is site-mixed. Small amounts can be made in a wheelbarrow or on a mixing board, but a half-bag power mixer does the job more quickly and easily. One with electric or gasoline power can be rented for a few dollars a day or can be purchased for less than $150. If much work is anticipated, having your own machine will be economical. A year ago I purchased an electric mixer for $130. After building four walks, three retaining walls, two curbs, and one patio, I sold it for $60. My operating costs were one quarter the price of a comparative rental.

Mixing is not mysterious. The infallible system is to buy dry-mixed concrete (in about 100-pound sacks of premeasured cement, sand, and gravel), but since each sack makes only 4 square feet of paving, it is seldom economical. Mixing from scratch is better. Sacked concrete is available everywhere; sand and gravel are sold separately or as "concrete mix," a ready combination of the proper amounts. The mix is easiest to control and generally costs little more than the two separate materials.

For mixing single ingredients, the standard formulas for garden pavement are 1-2-3 and 1-3-3: 1 part concrete, 2 parts sand, and 3 parts gravel, or 1 part concrete and 3 parts each of sand and gravel.

If you prefer to work with a combined mix as I do, a 1-4 or 1-5 proportion is recommended: 1 part concrete to 4 or 5 of mixed sand and gravel. Each formula will require 3 to 5 gallons of water. For 100 square feet of 4-inch paving, you will need approximately 8 sacks of cement and 18 cubic feet of sand-and-gravel mix. See Chart II, "Quantities and Coverage of Ingredients for Concrete," and Chart III, "Concrete Finishing," at end of this chapter.

Asphalt

Commonly called blacktop and long used for commercial and civic purposes, asphalt is a moderately liquid petroleum product that hardens on exposure to air. Now it is available as do-it-yourself material, and like concrete is laid down on a bed of gravel to make a hard pad. Many designers like to contrast it with other materials.

The familiar asphalt is the hot-mix you see applied in road construction. To use it requires substantial equipment and expertise. A second type is a cold-mix that relies on a chemical "cut-back" or an emulsion sometimes called water-soap to keep the asphalt soft and workable. When the chemical evaporates it leaves a hardened surface. The rate of evaporation is controlled by the type and proportion of chemical. There are currently sixteen mixtures of cut-back and five of emulsion, each graded according to curing time—fast, medium, or slow.

Improperly mixed or inadequately compacted asphalt can soften in moderate heat, and even when properly compounded can become uncomfortably warm on hot days. But on the plus side, it won't bounce heat as does concrete, and cools quickly when doused with water. It is faster and more economical to use than concrete.

A 600-foot section 4 feet wide can be poured, compacted, and smoothed in half a day, and less material is required than with concrete. A 1-inch topping over a good gravel base is often adequate for a walk, and a 2-inch layer for a drive. Properly laid, asphalt is as durable as concrete and easier to repair. Perhaps the sole objection to cold-mix (not hot) is the prolonged curing time. As much as six months must elapse before furniture with sharp feet can be placed on it, although you can walk on the surface immediately. This handicap can be minimized if you apply the mix in the fall: The surface can then harden by spring. Also, while cold-mix is ideal for do-it-yourself workers, it is not available in every area.

Poured asphalt is a good alternative. It looks like oil, pours like water, and is sold in 5-gallon containers. Begin with a 1- or 2-inch layer of medium gravel. Rake, level, moisten, and roll. Let the gravel dry, then pour asphalt from the can. An even flow of pouring may require practice, and you might do better with a rented spray. A spray does the job easily and professionally.

Add asphalt at the rate of 1½ to 1¾ gallons per square yard of surface. Let it stand for twenty-four hours, then repeat with a lighter application, ¼ to ½ gallon for the same area. Cover with pea gravel or coarse sand and roll with a weighted roller. Success depends on active rolling. Do it quickly and thoroughly, repeating until the surface is level and hard. Add sand, gravel, or asphalt as needed. Never begin a project if the weather is threatening. Until a walk has been sanded, rolled, and cured, water can cause extensive damage.

See Chart IV, "Applying Cold-Mix Asphalt," at end of this chapter.

Brick

Anyone willing to devote time and effort—the work can be slow and arduous—is assured of first-class results with brick. It is durable, easy to use, and capable of many handsome effects. The only real problem may be the difficulty of choice. To a beginner the varieties of brick are astonishing. The color range alone is considerable, for the least change in clay or baking time creates a noticeable if subtle shift in color. Bricks are sold in several variations of red, ebony, buff, and off-white. The wide range of textures compounds the problem, and of course texture affects the apparent color. Scraping, brushing, and scoring raw surfaces create patterns from smooth through "bark" (resembling a tree) to stripes (fine lines etched across the face). Half a dozen sizes complicate your decision.

If this were not enough, bricks are also classified on the basis of type and weathering ability. Currently there are four types:

PAVER.   One of the more expensive, a dense brick fired long for strength and resistance to cracking. Used when strength and durability are required, as for areas of heavy traffic and problem retaining walls.

FACE.   Another premium brick, costly because it is strong and uniform in color and size with few defects. Chosen for its strength and uniformity—for walks, retaining walls, and structures.

BUILDING OR COMMON BRICK.   Has good strength but less uniformity. Dimensions, for example, may vary as much as ¼ inch. Suitable for walls and walks, the variations in size giving character and, in time, a mellow look.

FIRE.   Designed to resist heat. While this brick was developed for industry, it is ideal for lining outdoor fireplaces and barbecue pits.

Weathering in bricks is in good part the ability to withstand moisture. The firing time affects the rate of absoprtion. Short-fired bricks absorb moisture readily and are subsequently susceptible to damage from freezing as the trapped water hardens, expands, and causes either cracks or surface flaking, a condition called spalling. Long-firing reduces porosity and minimizes absorption. There are now three classifications:

SW (Severe Weathering) A premium brick, long-fired, with minimum porosity. Best for moist, cold areas.

MW (Moderate Weathering) Standard firing with resistance to light freezing. A common choice for many jobs.

NW (No Weathering) Short-fired brick with little frost resistance. An economy choice where weather permits. Common bricks are available in all grades. Fire and Pavers are sold in SW only. Face bricks are generally available in SW and MW.

Cost. Brick can cost from $60 to $180 per thousand. Price depends on quality and uniformity, strength and weathering being the premium items of cost. You save money when you buy only those a job really requires. For most garden projects, you are safe with a lightly frost-resistant brick of minimal uniformity, i.e., the building brick, as strong as more expensive kinds yet costing as much as $50 less per thousand. Further savings can result when you buy in quantities of a thousand or more. The manufacturers' and dealers' highest costs are in storage, handling, and shipping.

Used brick may offer another opportunity for savings, but the economy depends upon several factors. Old brick must be cleaned, and the value of that job can be measured in time. If a dealer does the work, used brick may cost more than new; if you do the job, it may demand many more hours work than is profitable. Small amounts of mortar may enhance the appearance without affecting utility, but large amounts must be removed, and the only way is by chipping—a tedious hand process. Although surface scratches and old mortar make used brick especially attractive for informal features, the mortar may rule out the reliable bond you get from new brick. Hence, where strength is essential, used brick may not be satisfactory. Old bricks are in short supply, and some manufacturers convert new to "old" by chipping and splashing with mortar. While there is little visual difference, manufactured used brick generally costs more than the real kind.

See Chart V, "Brick Dimensions," and Chart VI, "Types of Brick," at end of this chapter.

Sand is recommended as a base for most brick walks and patios because it is easy and economical, but where freezing is a consideration, other bases may be more reliable. A brick-over-sand walk can buckle after heavy frost. Dry mortar is safe under moderate conditions. Where freezing is severe, brick should be laid over concrete.

The photographs at the end of this chapter illustrate some of the patterns in which brick can be laid. If possible, plan the width of the walk to accommodate the bricks. When determining the width, measure with a minimum of cutting.

Although you can cut with a brick hammer or cold chisel, a brickset is recommended because it is accurate and inexpensive (less than five dollars). Lay the brick on a stable base, then place the brickset at the line to be cut, beveled edge away from the section you will use. Strike the tool with a hammer and, when the brick cracks, dress any unevenness with an abrasive stone or another brick.

Spilled mortar is easily cleaned if you tackle it promptly. Moistened burlap makes a good scrubber and will remove even partially hardened material quickly, but once mortar sets it can only be removed chemically. The best cleaner consists of 9 parts water and 1 part muriatic acid. Rinse the area with a hose, apply the acid with a brush, scrub until the mortar dissolves, then rinse to prevent staining. Wear rubber gloves and use a plastic bucket. Test the effects of the acid first on a discarded brick.

A white deposit called efflorescence may appear after bricks have been wetted. The deposit is a water-soluble salt that rises from the brick or its base. It can be removed by brushing but not by water. Moisture will only drive the salt into the brick, and then the salt will reappear.

Adobe brick

As one architect said, "In the West, adobe is at the bottom of everyone's list because he has seen crumbling missions," but today's adobe differs from that of the early days. It includes asphalt stabilizers to give year-round durability and will last a lifetime. Uneven textures and warm, friendly tones make it pleasant for informal walks and walls. Although not available in as many sizes, grades, and textures as brick, adobe is versatile. It is laid in the manner of brick, usually over a bed of sand, but with a slightly wider joint.

Other materials

Loose aggregates—such as gravel, crushed rock, and decomposed granites—and woods—such as bark, chips, and rounds—are good for low-traffic areas. Although many are considered only temporary covers, you may find them interesting and attractive enough to renew.

Gravel and crushed rock are popular choices. They are most durable over a base of packed rock, such as decomposed granite, and most reliable between headers (wooden edgings that define the walk and confine the material), but they can be used successfully alone. Either way, choose ½- to ¾-inch rock and lay it 1 to 2 inches deep. Smaller rock works into the ground quickly. Larger rock may be difficult to walk on. A thinner layer may deteriorate fast. A thicker one may be too soft for easy walking, especially for women with high heels, open-toed shoes, or sandals. Apply the rock in thin layers: ½ inch is best. Rake, moisten, and roll. Repeat until built up to the proper depth.

Decomposed granite compacts well when moistened and rolled; granite can be built into a hard surface that neither flakes nor dusts. Crushed rock acts the same way, but is more expensive. Basically a roofing material, crushed rock is soft, breakable, and not suited to constant use. A clay called red rock is available in many cases. It becomes hard-packed after repeated rollings and can be used alone or as a base for gravel, concrete, or asphalt.

Several wood products are used for paving. Bark and wood chips are popular. Neither is affected by moisture, and when worn down can be added to the compost heap or worked directly into the soil. A ton covers 150 to 180 square feet. Though not suited to heavy traffic, wood products have many decorative possibilities for paths. Like gravel, they hold up longest when confined between headers.

Rounds—with their interesting texture, shape, and color—can make very attractive paths and small terraces. Redwood, cedar, and cypress last longest, but local woods can be used, and garden shops sell many kinds precut, with and without bark. If you have a chain saw, you can make your own. They should be at least 1 foot in diameter and 3 inches thick. Rounds that size or larger organize easily and provide a sturdy base for furniture. Smaller sizes will be visually too busy and are often unstable.

Most woods should be treated with a preservative. Pentachloro-phenal is recommended and is available from most lumberyards. It is often mixed with mineral spirits. Directions, which vary, are on the containers. The treatment will not stain most woods, although a few— oak being one—may temporarily turn purple.

To lay rounds, excavate 6 to 8 inches below the proposed surface, then level the area. Provide drainage as required. Frame the perimeter with 1 x 6 boards, then spread 4 inches of sand. Level with a screed or rake. Position the rounds one by one, hitting each with a wooden block and mallet to settle it. Check each top to make sure it is flat and on the same level as the others. Then fill the intervening spaces with sand or crushed stone; ½- to ¾-inch stone is recommended because it retains its shape well after it is tamped.

Steps

An obvious and often necessary means of changing levels, steps can be made of wood, brick, stone, concrete, earth, or combinations of these. In a formal area the most effective steps match or carefully contrast with walks and walls. For example, in an opening of a brick retaining wall, steps are best all brick or with a brick face and concrete or flagstone treads. Concrete steps can be formal or informal, depending on shape and texture. An aggregate finish is less formal than a smooth one, and when combined with rough brick risers, it is still less formal. Wooden risers with earth or grass treads give a natural look.

Steps are measured by the tread, the width of the portion on which you step, and the riser, the height between treads. The scale outdoors is exaggerated when compared with indoor steps. As a rule, the smaller the riser the greater the tread.

Step and Riser Relationship

RISER HEIGHT IN INCHES	TREAD DEPTH IN INCHES
4	20
4½	18
5	16
5½	15
6	14
6½	13
7	11–12

These figures indicate the most common relationships, but they can be changed to suit your land. One landscape architect considers a 20-inch tread and 4-inch riser the ideal combination for a garden. Another claims that a 17-inch tread and 5-inch riser is better. There are no absolute rules, but few outdoor steps should have a tread of less than 11 inches and a riser of more than 7 inches. If steps are really necessary on a steep slope in limited space, treads will have to be narrower, risers slightly higher. An average step, one considered workable for children and adults, has a 5½- to 6-inch riser and a 15-inch tread. A leisurely ramp effect calls for very wide treads and minimal risers. A 25- to 30-inch tread and 4-inch riser are possible under such conditions.

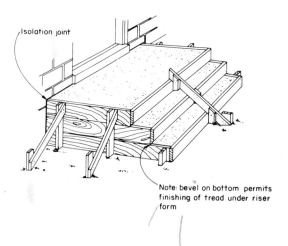

Isolation joint

Note: bevel on bottom permits finishing of tread under riser form

CONCRETE STEPS

Poured-concrete steps are easily made with a form built up of 2 x 4s as shown. Temporary support at sides and front is essential. It is also necessary to insulate the poured steps from existing structure. This can be done with asphalt-impregnated building paper.

(Courtesy of Portland Cement Association)

Bridges

Once built only to span gulleys and water for convenient communication, bridges now are sometimes introduced into a landscape primarily for an aesthetic or psychological effect. A bridge can extend the line of a walk, increasing the apparent depth of the garden. Another may relieve the monotony of an extensive level area. Some serve as ramps or take the place of steps, for bridges need not be level or equally based at both ends.

My own property is divided by a stream, over which a bridge connects my office with my home. At Lake Tahoe a half-bridge, half-step structure follows the slope downward to a house at lake level, solving a difficult problem of grade. Not far away, another resident has built a bridge from his back porch to a hillside for access to land otherwise unusable. Another man has a bridge as an entry from a parking lot. It is level with the second story, the main living floor of his house; and only the bridge makes this plan feasible.

Bridges need sturdy support. Generally heavy timbers or concrete piers supply this. The walkway supports should be equally rugged to minimize bounce: 4 x 6 or 4 x 8 timbers are recommended for most spans, and for long ones steel I-beams may be better. When there is any doubt about stress or strength, consult an architect or engineer.

Be sure to gear the height of the bridge to the heaviest flow of the stream. Placid streams that never rise with winter rains can be spanned with large stones or a low walkway. But where a seasonal runoff may occur or a storm double the stream's width and height, you must allow for it in the walkway. My own bridge is 7 feet above low stream level because the water can rise nearly that much in winter.

A railing is generally advisable, especially when the walkway is narrow. You can keep it visually light with lightweight materials or well-separated stanchions. The basic design can be harmonized with your house by employing the same lumber as that of the house or repeating an element of its design. The feeling of security can be enhanced by increasing the width of the walkway. Safety at night may make lighting imperative.

Chart II   Quantities and Coverage of Ingredients for Concrete

This chart indicates the amounts required for any project and thus also shows whether the amounts can be transported personally or will require delivery.

(Courtesy of Portland Concrete Association)
A 1:2¼:3 mix = 1 part cement to 2¼ parts sand
to 3 parts 1-in. max. aggregate

CONCRETE REQUIRED cu. ft.	CEMENT* lb.	MAX. AMOUNT OF WATER TO USE gal.		SAND lb.	COARSE AGGREGATE lb.
		U.S.	IMPERIAL		
1	24	1¼	1	52	78
3	71	3¾	3⅛	156	233
5	118	6¼	5¼	260	389
6¾ (¼ cu. yd.)	165	8	6¾	350	525
13½ (½ cu. yd.)	294	16	13½	700	1,050
27 (1 cu. yd.)	588	32	27	1,400	2,100

*U.S. bag of cement weighs 94 pounds. Canadian bag of cement weighs 80 pounds.

Chart III   Concrete Finishing

FINISH	PROCEDURE	COMMENT
Smooth	Use a steel trowel. After the concrete has partially hardened, work the trowel over the surface several times, beginning lightly. A deluxe finish may require three or four trowelings.	The easiest to maintain, the most difficult to make.
Wood-float	Use a mason's float, a wooden trowel. Level the concrete with the screed, then let it harden slightly. Work the surface with the float to bring the moisture to the top.	The surface is smooth enough to be serviceable, yet not as slick as the first. Accords well with many garden designs.
Broom	Screed the concrete, then float lightly to seal the surface. Let it partially harden, then roughen with broom. Designs depend upon whether you work the broom straight across, in circles, or in other designs.	Visually interesting. Roughened texture reduces surface glare and increases traction. Often used for steps and ramps. Although a dust-catcher, it can be easily cleaned with water.
Rake	Variation of the broom surface, made in a similar manner with either a bamboo or metal-tined garden rake.	Increased traction, reduced glare. The pattern, while aggressive, is interesting.
Exposed aggregate	Concrete is leveled and then floated for surface smoothness. Let it harden slightly, then flush with the angled spray of a hose, brushing gently to remove surface concrete. You can start with a broom and use a smaller brush to touch up.	A popular finish, having a natural, aged appearance. Pebbly surface blends with many garden details. Several colors are possible. If you specify an "aggregate mix," you can choose white, gray, or black rock.

FINISH	PROCEDURE	COMMENT
Pattern	Designs can be pressed into the semihardened surface as with a cooky mold. Stampers can be cut from plywood.	Complete latitude for a unique pavement pattern.
Flagstone	Similar to the last. Random flagstone pattern is imitated by drawing flagstone design on partially hardened concrete with a metal jointer or groover. An alternate method is to use a series of wood patterns cut from ¼ x 1½-inch lattice stock. Edges can be made jagged to simulate flagstone. Press into partially hardened concrete, then float the surface around the edges for smoothness. Let harden, then remove. Fill depressions with mortar to suggest authenticity.	
Color	Cement can be colored by painting after it hardens or by the addition of pigments as it is laid. Mineral oxide pigments produce the most durable finish. For brilliant colors, use white Portland cement. Coloring can be mixed with the cement or applied as a topping in a "dry shake," spread on the surface with a swinging motion—almost as you sow grain. For best results, spread half the required amount, float the surface, then repeat.	

Chart IV   Applying Cold-Mix Asphalt

Cold-mix can be a do-it-yourself project if you live close to a mixing plant; otherwise you may need a trailer. Most firms are geared to professional needs and will not deliver small amounts. For 100 square feet of asphalt you will need:

  1½ tons crushed rock (1- to 1½-inch diameter)
  ½ ton fine rock (¼- to ¾-inch diameter)
  ½ ton cold-mix, either cut-back or emulsion type

APPLICATION STEP	PROCEDURE
1. Preparation	Scrape topsoil to firm ground. Excavate to required depth. Level or grade and check drainage.
2. Sterilization	Sterilize soil before applying asphalt to prevent "grow-through." Apply sterilant according to directions. Rock salt can work, but better job is done by commercial products, such as polyborchlorate, arsenic trioxide, or Borascule.
3. Construction	Set the headers in place. Use wood closest size to depth required, 1 x 4, 1 x 6, etc. Adjust pieces so upper edge is the finished surface. Secure well to anchored posts.
4. Application, base rock	Apply a 2- to 4-inch layer of large stone (1"–1½"). Level with a screed or rake; then work with a roller. A water-filled roller will do a good job.
5. Application, small rock	Follow with a layer of fine stone (¼"–¾"). Work into the spaces between larger stones. This step should be done with care. Eventually the smaller rock will bind with the large and with the asphalt to create an interlocked pad. Roll thoroughly.
6. Wetting	Moisten the rock well to improve compaction. If you use an emulsion-type mix, the rock can be asphalted slightly damp. If you use a cut-back mix, the rock should be completely dry.

APPLICATION STEP	PROCEDURE
7. Application, cold-mix	Shovel cold-mix over the compacted rock. Rake to a 1-inch depth. If you use cut-back mix, prime the rock first with a light coating of liquid asphalt.
8. Compaction	Roll the surface well, wait two to three hours, then repeat. The walk is now ready for traffic. Do not place sharp-footed furniture on the surface for four to six months.

Chart V   Brick Dimensions

Dealers may refer to brick as of nominal or actual size. *Nominal* is the brick's dimensions plus a ¼-inch mortar joint. *Actual* size is just that, the actual size.

NAME	WIDTH IN INCHES	HEIGHT IN INCHES	LENGTH IN INCHES
Standard	4	2⅔	8
Economy	4	4	8
Roman	4	2	12
Norman	4	2⅔	12
Utility	4	4	12
Split	4	1½	8

Chart VI Types of Brick

Name	Sizes	Average Cost per Thousand	Comment
Paver	Standard	$150–$175	Rounded edges, minimum porosity. Excellent for heavy-traffic areas, walls, general construction. Relatively smooth finish, easy to clean.
Split Paver	Split	$145–$165	Used over a concrete base for paving, also for walls and light construction.
Common Split	Split	$70–$115	Facing, paving, general-traffic areas.
Wire-cut Common	All	$55–$100	Good for light traffic, walls, and general construction.
Wire-cut Clinker	Standard, Roman, and Norman	$85–$115	Long-fired to increase hardness. Distinctive discoloration has decorative value.
Buff	All	$100–$160	Light-colored, hard-fired. For paving, walls, and general construction. Excellent for edging.
Face	All	$80–$140	Minimum porosity, hard surface, uniformity in each size. Good when these qualities are wanted. Paving, walks, and general construction.
Sand-molded	Standard, but slightly larger on face because it is turned from a mold.	$80–$140	Smooth texture, easy to clean.

Poured concrete is generally contained within wooden forms until it hardens, the form creating a well-defined edge. The cement in this picture is transit-mixed.

A screed, simply a length of 2 x 4, strikes off or levels the mixture with the top of the form. Board should reach across the form. A small roll of fine material may build up in front of the screed. It can be scooped away and used in a depressed spot. A stiffer mixture may require two passes.

Rounded corners are best made with roofing tin or thin plywood. Secure the forms with upright stakes. Concrete for walks does not need reinforcement; for steps it does. Ten-gauge steel mesh is good—floated midway in the mixture.

Concrete is tamped with "jitterbug," a metal form with a screen on the bottom. Tamping works heavier rock deep into the mix, leaves finer rock near the surface, which makes finishing easier. Jitterbug can be rented.

A plastic or wooden float brings the smoother, finer materials to the surface. Work in circular sweeps in both directions so float marks overlap. Do not over-work: Too much floating will bring up excess moisture and fine sand, called "fat," producing a thin, easily cracked surface.

Preliminary edging is next, easily done with an edging tool in a series of short back-and-forth motions. Two or more passes now, and one after cement is partially hardened, will yield a professional edge.

For nonskid surface, work a broom over the concrete after floating. Coarseness of broom and depth of scratching determine degree of roughness. A light motion produces an unobtrusive but effective surface. After brushing, use an edging tool to remove the brush effect from a narrow strip (1 inch or so) along the edge.

Aggregate surface is made by washing and brushing partially hardened cement. Use a concentrated (but not too forceful) spray. Brush with a broom at same time. For stubborn areas, take a whisk or hand broom and use a more concentrated spray.

After concrete hardens, forms can be removed or left as part of the design. Here the retained form accentuates the transition between lawn and walk. Mayfair Homes

Curbing form can be made of any stiff wood wide enough for the job, but when curves are involved, plywood is best. Thin metal may not hold the form. Plywood is bent by "kerfing," a series of cuts that weaken but do not sever the wood. Forms must be supported frequently along sides by pipe or wood.

Curbing must be well supported to prevent shifting as the mix is poured. Uprights and angled supports keep weaker areas aligned.

Top edge of form lumber must be properly leveled since it represents the final surface of the concrete. Level and check at several points.

Steps require well-supported forms. Check the corners for square, and side pieces for plumb.

A handsome drive features stripes of smooth and exposed aggregate surfaces. Lloyd Bond, L.A.

A semismooth surface with stones purposely exposed at intervals. U.C.L.A.

A series of textures in formal squares creates an interesting walk. Mayfair Homes

Flagstone is the aristocrat of paving materials and as durable and permanent as it looks. It can be laid on the ground and over sand, but is best when set over concrete. Edging of stones increases the informal effect. U.C.L.A.

Paving materials combined: bands of light-colored rock, stone, and dark river rock for the walk, edging, and drain beside a wooden porch. U.C.L.A.

A service path both practical and attractive. Gravel edging against wall absorbs drip of rain, and between concrete slabs avoids need for mowing.

Distinguished combination of textures: a high concrete pad with incised edging, a bed of rock, and a concrete walk. Surfaces are semismooth so they will not dominate against the rock. Eriksson, Peters & Thoms, L.A.

A buffer zone of rock between lawn and smooth-textured walk. Holiday Inn, Gallup, N. Mex.

Stepping stones across an open lawn do not affect the sense of serenity. Uniformity and spacing of the slabs produce a light, floating design. Marc Askew, designer

A variation of the same concept obtained by carefully positioned exposed aggregate. Lawn breaks the fullness of the cement. Marc Askew, designer

Readymade concrete rounds are easy to lay—on leveled ground or on a sand base. They are inviting and informal between a border of ivy. Garden of Mr. and Mrs. Montgomery Fisher

A precisely constructed rock wall, with a well-planned path on a field of moss, edges a parking area. Residence of Mr. and Mrs. Arthur Shapiro. Jocelyn Domela, L.A.

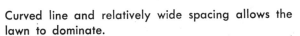

Curved line and relatively wide spacing allows the lawn to dominate.

Trees can be preserved within a walk if wells are formed to provide for growth and watering. La Posada Inn, La Paz, Baja Sur, Mexico

For best service a brick walk must be laid on a drained foundation. The easiest base is sand. Excavate 2 to 4 inches below the thickness of the brick, fill with sand to proper depth, level with a screed, and position the bricks. A pattern with the least amount of cutting will make work move faster.

Level each brick, then pound for a solid base. Surface must agree with those of other bricks. To maintain a constant grade, use a level.

Showing the three steps in laying a brick wall—excavation, base of sand, and positioned brick.

A good path can be made by leaving brick loose over sand or by filling the cracks, but for a stronger walk, use mortar. Pour on dry mortar and brush into cracks. A hand brush or broom offers greatest control.

Work water into the cracks, over the mortar. Use a hose with a low spray or a broom and tub. Do not overwater. Remove mortar from surface to prevent staining.

Herringbone pattern on the left; basket weave on the right. Open edges of herringbone can be left or filled with cut brick or cement.

Herringbone pattern with mortar joint. The inset joint can be made with a bricklayer's jointer or with the edge of a pipe. The standard joint is ½ inch.

Familiar bond-on-bond design with alternating joints and an edging of exposed aggregate.

Herringbone design with an edge of straight-laid brick. The contrast is formal and effective.

96

Divide large areas with headers to make work easier. Brick in foreground has open seams; in background, mortar-filled joints. Lloyd Bond, L.A.

A full patio of brick in basket weave set on sand. With dry mortar, it is solid enough for automobiles.

Herringbone pattern leads the eye down a well-defined path. Golden Gate Center. Lawrence Halprin, L.A.

Informal paving of brick set over sand and not touching so grass can grow between. Solid timber makes perfect boundary seat. Thomas D. Church, L.A.

In a desert setting lengths of old wood as stepping stones go beautifully with gravel and succulent plants. Los Angeles County Arboretum

Medium-size gravel forms the base and roughly defines the area; larger stepping stones make walking easy and establish the route. Holiday Inn

A straightforward gravel walk between wooden headers leads down a slope, the rigid line softened by prostrate junipers.

Natural stepping stones set in earth, with minute creeping plants and a border of lush turf, create a walk that seems to be a part of the land. U.C.L.A.

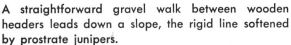

Asphalt is well adapted for use with other materials, as with square concrete pavers framed in wood. Strybing Arboretum

A hard-packed cinder walk can handle considerable traffic. Headers prevent this one from impinging on lawn. Marc Askew, designer

Railroad ties cut in short sections make an effective curbing. For permanence they are best set in concrete. Los Angeles County Arboretum

Octagonal sections of wood set on end hold the soil and define a planted area. Strybing Arboretum

Another view of the edging shown above right.

Simple wooden steps, the treads nailed to stringers. Construction is easy, the result reliable. Richard A. Campbell, A.I.A.

(Left) These stairs are more involved: wooden stringers mounted over steel, with wooden treads and metal railings. Residence of Mr. and Mrs. Arthur J. Priestly. (Right) Gravel steps are most easily made by confining rock between wooden headers, and best on a gentle slope where risers can be low and headers do not need much reinforcement.

Deep treads of railroad timber given a somewhat formal look next to wide brick walls. Garden of Mr. and Mrs. Harold Hecht. Jocelyn Domela, L.A.

Large bridge timbers are of good size for outdoor steps. Most reliable when set in concrete, they can also be secured with driftpins—large metal spikes set through at angles. Here delightful between rock walls. Thomas D. Church, L.A.

Concrete slabs, floated through a mounting to the wall, achieve an airy, weightless effect. Each unit repeats the larger pad at bottom. Lytton Center

Steps made of 2 x 6 risers and concrete treads edged with plants are unusual and charming. Eckbo, Dean, Austin and Williams, L.A.

Natural stone steps must be of the proper shape and size. Junipers are skillfully used to tie all together. Residence of Mr. and Mrs. Arthur Shapiro. Jocelyn Domela, L.A.

An interesting flight of wood rounds set in an asphalt ramp. Mayfair Homes

Concrete slabs well designed for entranceway, and well supported. Built-in lights assure safety. Residence of Mr. and Mrs. Arthur J. Priestly

Simple steps with long lines and low risers lead to a quiet and private place. Small pool and fountain heighten the mood. Garden of Mr. and Mrs. Irving Hammer

Traditional brick is a formal material. These steps retain the styling of the wall. Eckbo, Dean, Austin and Williams, L.A.

Concrete steps need reinforcement—generally steel. Scored edges and nonslip surface, such as exposed aggregate, make for safety. Square riser-and-tread combination is suitable for this service area. Residence of Mr. and Mrs. Arthur J. Priestly

Field rock and flagstone in friendly harmony. Concrete also forms a compatible part. U.C.L.A.

Lava-rock steps against a retaining wall of the same material. Steps are set over concrete for durability.

Rock employed on a grand scale makes an imposing design. Here stones, smaller river rock, and concrete combine for an effect of naturalness and strength. U.C.L.A.

Rough stones and logs make these steps appear natural and they accommodate changes in grade. Gravel treads throughout give unity. U.C.L.A.

Bridges can be a necessity or a decoration. Wide bridges do not require railings. U.C.L.A.

The design of this narrow bridge slows the pace to allow time to enjoy surroundings. Garden of Mrs. Gretchen Plechner. Joseph Copp, Jr., L.A.

Japanese bridge with a beautifully simple railing. Planking runs the width of the bridge to allow flexibility in construction. Sea World

A typical Japanese rock bridge. Made from cut stone, expensive and difficult to find, it can be simulated with poured concrete. Make a form over a slow-moving stream, support well, pour the mixture in one piece, reinforce with steel rod. Sea World

A Japanese bridge simply made of 2 x 12 planking staggered to slow the visitor. Sea World

A bridge where none is needed may add flair and excitement. This bridge leads to a play area. Mayfair Homes

A bridge over a wash gives a sense of water and space. Concrete was poured into carefully assembled form, and wash was created where there was none before. Braemar Homes. Armstrong and Sharfman, L.A.

Another bridge creates a sense of water. Braemar Homes. Armstrong and Sharfman, L.A.

Stepping stones are practical for crossing quiet waters. Rounds were obtained from a Japanese flour mill; rectangles were cut for the garden. Both can be duplicated with concrete. U.C.L.A.

6

Fences and Gates

In today's close-packed society a fence or wall is becoming more and more desirable, for privacy and some degree of protection. Primarily, fences define boundaries. In landscape design they create backgrounds, dividers, and supports for vines. On the practical side, fences largely control the effects of sun, sound, and wind.

The weight and the height of any fence are most important. Obviously it should not appear either overweight or unstable. Proper height is determined by purpose, common sense, and terrain. To shut out an unpleasant view or traffic or a public walk, a fence must be high—but cautiously so. While height may ensure privacy, it may also create a sense of confinement, especially in a small area. In scale for the purpose may be out of scale for the terrain.

The design of your house and grounds will generally suggest the appropriate type of fencing. Post and rail are excellent for ranch-style houses. White pickets are associated with colonial dwellings. Louvers offer privacy with ventilation. An open fence is ideal for a small garden, often even making it appear larger. Board-on-board design is appropriate for boundary markers.

To create a shaded place wide enough to sit in, fencing will have to be high. Uninterrupted panels produce full shade. Cut-outs, slats, or expanded metal give a moving pattern of broken shade. Transparent plastic and textured glass reduce glare. Sounds can be partly muffled with solid panels and baffles, especially in conjunction with plantings of shrubs and trees.

Wind control is a less simple problem, as recent experiments indicate. Solid, louvered, and slat fences were tested in southern California, with results both predictable and unexpected. The solid fence was ineffective: Air lashed over the top like waves against a rock. But with a baffle added (a trick borrowed from marine architects), control was improved. The baffle worked well when angled with the wind, and even better when turned against it. The effectiveness of louvers depended on the direction of their slant. Louvers aimed groundward (toward the garden side) made the shaded area uncomfortably cool; when directed upward, the comfort improved and the area of control was widened.

The best-functioning design was the one least expected to be. A 5-foot-high fence of vertical slats provided surprising protection 15 feet away—a distance greater than that affected by other designs. The test engineer remarked, "The slats allow some wind through, and that is the secret. Wind is quickly dissipated through the openings, creating a layer of slow-moving air at ground level. It becomes a cushion that keeps the turbulent air from descending."

Adapt the results to your own fencing after a wind study on your property. The "prevailing" local wind may not be common to your land, because a house or garage can alter its direction. Hang strips of cloth or paper in several places and note their response under varying conditions.

Legal requirements

Most cities and some heavily populated counties have construction codes that cover fencing. Building permits are generally required. Some ordinances restrict the height of boundary fencing to 6 feet, and front-yard fences to 3 or 4 feet. Away from property lines, fencing can often be as low or as high as you like. Special problems may arise when fences are built on property lines. The structure can belong to both landowners as joint tenants, which means that the owners may have to share construction and maintenance costs. Other restrictions may be added to corner lots where fence height is reduced so oncoming motorists can see each other. A few communities also regulate the type of material and/or construction. Exceptions are usually limited to unincorporated areas.

Normally you can fence or not, as you choose, but in some situations you may be required to. In most areas livestock must be enclosed. When your place has an "attractive nuisance," a swimming pool, pond, or excavation, the municipality may require security fencing—a chain-link or equivalent. In some townships a security fence or masonry wall is required when property borders a freeway, canal, or railroad.

Problem places

A level lot offers few unexpected problems, but a hilly site can provide plenty. Save your sanity and time by anticipating trouble on paper. With detailed construction plans drawn in advance, problems become less formidable.

There are two ways to meet the challenge of a slope: Fencing can follow the changes in terrain or keep an independent level. The choice depends on the particular slope and on the fence material. As a rule a fence should harmonize with a nearby structure, but with the terrain when it is open. Thus fencing beside a house will be horizontal and as uniform in height as possible, no matter how complex its construction. Without that proximity, fencing can follow the terrain, either leveled or slanted as you wish. "Flexible" materials, such as screens, rails, and pickets, can follow the contours easily, but "stiff" ones, such as plywood panels and fitted boards, are usually built with the top horizontal and the sections stepped at intervals to fit the change in ground level.

When trees are to be preserved, fencing can be built to within an inch of the trunk, provided supports are far enough away to prevent root damage. The edges of a fence should be free and flexible to allow for cutting back as the tree trunk expands. Never use a tree as a post. Nails and screws puncture the bark, let insects and bacteria enter, and can invite disaster.

Streamside fencing requires a combination of imagination and common sense. On the one hand, posts should be placed far enough from the bank to anticipate erosion and washouts, and on the other, should be close enough to include as much territory as possible. In some situations, bankside plantings can reduce erosion and effect a compromise. Crossing water can be more difficult. While fencing over water should be low, it can become a catchall for debris. A fluctuating stream complicates the problem, and the one practical solution for that may be a floodgate—a barrier pivoted to swing upward with the volume of the water.

Materials

Wire, sheet metal, plastic, hardboard, glass, and even masonry have made good fences, but wood, alone or with other materials, has made by far the greater number. When you have learned how to build with wood you can easily control most other materials. Masonry construction is discussed in Chapter 7.

Ready-made fencing is available in many towns. It is generally made of wood, or wood and wire, and sometimes preassembled, but usually merely precut. Packaged in 6- to 10-foot sections, it avoids measuring, cutting, and the guesswork of cost. The range of material and design is limited. If you want a special combination of materials or unusual design you will have to build from scratch. This is not a formidable undertaking; the construction of fences is neither difficult nor demanding.

Redwood, cedar, and cypress are normally recommended because they are decay and borer-resistant, but the recommendations should be qualified. Only wood close to the heart is markedly resistant. Sapwood, that portion closer to the bark, is nearly as susceptible to rot as are other woods. And only fencing in direct contact with the soil requires full protection. When you want to economize, the fence can be made in other ways. You can combine two qualities of resistant wood, expensive heartwood where protection is needed, and less costly sapwood elsewhere. You can also use local softwoods. The choice depends chiefly on the way the wood is to be finished. If it will remain natural, unpainted, or with a clear finish, a single kind of wood is best to maintain a uniform grain and color. When a fence is painted, variations in material are concealed.

Softwoods to be buried should be made decay-resistant. Creosote, pentachlorophenal, and copper naphthenate are three good preservatives available under many brand names. Creosote is the most economical, but an area treated with it cannot be painted; a brown stain always works through. The other chemicals, slightly more expensive, are nonstaining. Pentachlorophenal is available as a preservative and as a preservative combined with a water repellent. The combination is excellent for wood that you want to weather naturally. Normally the chemical is applied to the parts of the post to be buried plus a band of 6 to 12 inches above ground to discourage borers. Some builders also add it to joints and corners on the weather side. The value of a preservative on heartwood is doubtful, because the fibers there are so dense that the wood absorbs little.

There is latitude in the way a fence can be assembled. But no matter how you proceed, an important factor of strength is in the size of the material used. Certain combinations of material and method have proved to be reliable, and these are the basis of the following recommendations.

POSTS.   In general, fences to 5 feet and picket-and-wire fences of most heights should have 4 x 4 or doubled 2 x 4 posts. Higher fences require 6 x 6 timbers. Posts for gates should be stronger, of 6 x 6 to 5 feet, and 8 x 8 when higher. If round timber is used, the diameter should be one size larger than for squared material. For example, a post 8 inches in diameter should be substituted for a 6 x 6 post.

For rigidity, fence posts are traditionally set into the ground, but they no longer need be. They can be bolted aboveground to metal stirrups set in concrete, a technique that speeds construction and increases durability. Supports can be fabricated at home or purchased ready-made from lumberyards. Two are required per post and should be set at least 6 inches in concrete. Quarter-inch bolts or larger should be used. Allow at least half an inch clearance between the post and concrete to keep the wood dry, prolonging its service.

When posts are sunk into the ground, the amount to be buried depends on the height. For a 6-foot post the buried end should measure 2 to 2½ feet. For taller posts the buried end should be 35 to 45 percent of the height, depending on the weight of the fence and the expected force of wind. Metal supports are used on security fences, such as chain-link types. In section, they are either round or "T." Some are notched to better hold the links. Having relatively greater strength than wooden posts, they are appreciably smaller in width. They should be sunk into the ground, to the same depths as stipulated for wood, above. For sinking metal in concrete, see Basic Construction (below).

RAILS. Standard lumber lengths range from 6 to 18 feet. The longer dimensions can be used when the wood is supported every 6 to 10 feet. For many projects 2 x 4s are satisfactory and are used as backing for pickets and panels. A heavy-duty fence may need hard-to-find rails, such as 3 x 4s, or other slightly thicker materials.

FACE BOARDS. Pickets are available in widths from 1½ to 6 inches and lengths from 2 to 5½ feet. Rustic slats, such as grape stakes, are usually 2 inches square in lengths of 3 to 8 feet. Cedar slats and bamboo are often wired together in rolls 8 to 10 feet long and 3 to 6 inches wide. Other possible facing wood are sold in 1-inch thickness and 4- to 10-inch widths. Thicker boards are seldom used except when maximum security is needed.

Plywood is sold in 4 x 8-foot panels. Half-inch-thick plywood is generally satisfactory; ¾-inch can be used when more strength is required. Be sure to specify "exterior grade." All wood, including plywood, is available in smooth and textured (unfinished) surfaces. Grooved lumber is not recommended, because fencing is exposed and the wood can expand and contract. It is better to allow ¼ to ½ inch of clearance between boards to accommodate movement.

Hardboard paneling has become popular for fences. If you could remove the factors you find annoying about wood—knots, splinters, and end grain—you would have hardboard, that is, reconstituted wood. The panels will not expand, buckle, or rot. They can be set very close; and they are primed, ready for painting. Most hardboards are available in many patterns, including filigrees and perforations.

Basic construction

Posts are generally erected 8 to 10 feet apart, but when the rails are thin or the fence unusually high, they should be closer, 6 feet in most locations and 4 feet in windy areas. If an exact starting corner is not evident, the first post position can be located through the use of batter boards, 2- or 3-foot 1 x 4s supported on stakes just above the ground. Strings are laid along the proposed fence lines and one end of each line is tied to a batter board. The point at which the lines intersect is the corner location.

RULE OF 3-4-5.   Wherever possible, it is desirable for two fences to meet at a perfect right angle. You can form this with a carpenter's square, but the angle should be double-checked. The best method is by the "rule of 3-4-5." On one string, measure 3 feet from the corner; on the other string measure 4 feet. Mark both points, then lay a line across the two strings. That distance from point to point should measure exactly 5 feet. If it does not, the corner is out of square. Move one or both of the strings until they conform. Leave the strings in place to align all the posts.

Posthole drainage is important. It keeps the buried sections dry and reduces the chance of rot. To provide drainage, holes are dug deeper than the buried post end. In average soils 6 to 12 inches more is adequate. In clays allow 16 to 24 inches. The diameter of a hole depends on the soil. In well-drained loam it need be only slightly wider than the post; in clay it should be 4 to 8 inches wider. Fill this extra excavation with gravel. When concrete is used, allow 6 to 12 inches around a wooden post. For a metal post the concrete should be at least 2 feet deep and 8 inches in diameter.

When the soil is relatively free of rocks, holes can be dug with an auger. The simplest type twists like a giant drill, lifting loose soil with the blades. A more recent type has shell-like cutters and is very good in sandy soil. In rocky soil you may need a clamshell digger, which is basically two shovels pivoted in the center. When you need many holes, a power digger will speed the work. There are two types of power digger: for one-man or two-man operation. All tools can be rented for a few dollars a day.

Do not vary posthole positions simply because the ground is easier to dig in another place. The strength (and beauty) of a fence depends on uniformity. Small rocks can be dug out and large ones can often be broken up. Soft rock can be broken with a sledge and removed in pieces. Harder ones may require a stonemason's "star drill," a special cross-hair chisel, and wedges called "feathers." When a rock is too large to be broken, posts can be attached with pins cemented to holes drilled in the rock.

Alignment should be checked before holes are filled. Check for plumb on two sides with a carpenter's level, then secure posts with bracing. Do not be concerned with top alignment at this point, but be certain only that posts are at least as high as dimensions require. Any excess can be removed after filling, and a full row can be quickly cut uniform. Tops may be leveled, but slanted, beveled, or rounded tops shed water better, safeguarding the post.

Building gates

Normally a gate conforms to the design and material of the fence, but it need not do so if special considerations, such as emphasis or unusual width come into play. In walls of brick or concrete, gates must be made of other materials. However, as a matter of taste and judgment, the design should be in character.

The size of a gate is determined partly by its purpose and partly by the height of the fence. A high fence requires a high gate. A security fence and gate must be high. A narrow gate may be practical for a seldom-used walk, but a wider one is best where there is considerable traffic. A very wide one may look pretentious, and possibly too heavy for its supports. A 3-foot opening is considered minimal, and 40 to 48 inches more feasible. To assure easy opening, the frame should be ½ to 1 inch narrower than the distance between gateposts. In most cases 2 x 4 or 2 x 6 framing is adequate. The frame must be square, and the corners should be checked as parts are assembled. Bracing prevents sagging, and in most cases a tightly fitted 2 x 4 is adequate. When a gate receives rough treatment, as from children, it is well to use a wire and turnbuckle, which allow for continuing adjustments. Turnbuckles, twistable tensioners, are available in several sizes from hardware stores and lumberyards.

Proper hinges are essential. The commonest cause of sagging is hinges too small, too few, or secured with too small screws. Use hinges as strong as possible for the design and size of the gate. It may be impossible to mount a heavy-duty strap hinge to a gate with a narrow frame or little backing. But you may be able to add an extra hinge. For any gate, three hinges are usually better than two; a heavy gate may require four.

There are more than a dozen types of latches. In some cases the gate must be designed to accommodate the latch. Do not complete your design without knowing what kind and size of latch you will use. For a rustic appearance a homemade sliding bar is practical. For real security you need a latch that can be locked. For children an easy-to-open latch is best, and for small children, spring-operated, self-closing hinges that avoid the need for a latch. You should investigate all of the possibilities.

FENCE AND GATE CONSTRUCTION
(Drawings by courtesy of California Redwood Association)

On slopes, solid or louvered fences should be stepped.

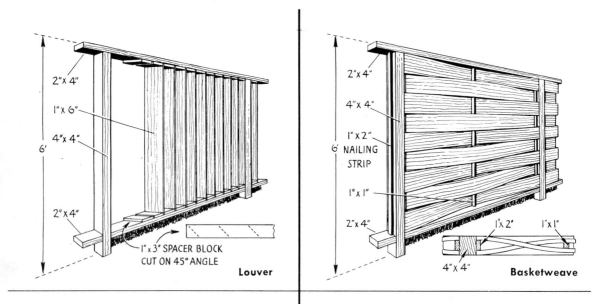

Louver

Basketweave

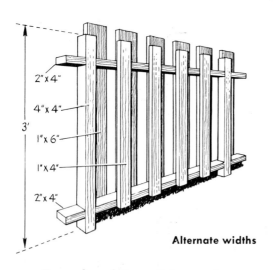

Alternate widths

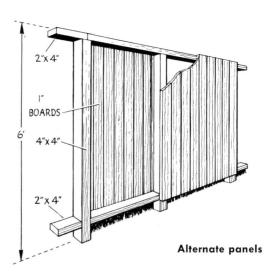

Alternate panels

Examples of "open" fences that create light and shadow, control the wind, or offer a feeling of depth.

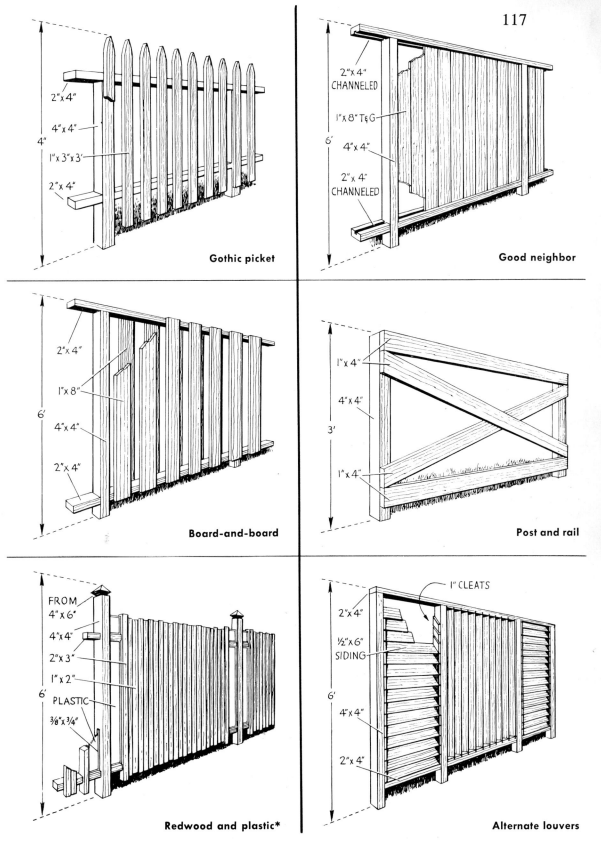

Gothic picket

2" x 4"
4" x 4"
1" x 3" x 3'
2" x 4"
4"

Good neighbor

2" x 4" CHANNELED
1" x 8" T&G
4" x 4"
2" x 4" CHANNELED
6'

Board-and-board

2" x 4"
1" x 8"
4" x 4"
2" x 4"
6'

Post and rail

1" x 4"
4" x 4"
1" x 4"
3'

Redwood and plastic*

FROM 4" x 6"
4" x 4"
2" x 3"
1" x 2"
PLASTIC
3⁄8" x 3⁄4"
6'

Alternate louvers

1" CLEATS
2" x 4"
1⁄2" x 6" SIDING
4" x 4"
2" x 4"
6'

Other examples of fence designs.

How to set fence posts

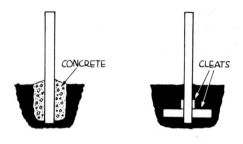

(Left) In concrete. (Right) In earth secured with a cleat at right angles.

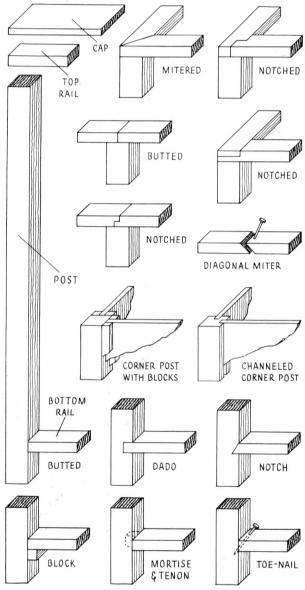

Rails and caps, the major supports and parts of a fence, can be set against the posts in various ways. The simplest is the block support, *bottom left*. Other examples show a more fitted construction. Panels can be attached with blocks or in grooves cut into the posts.

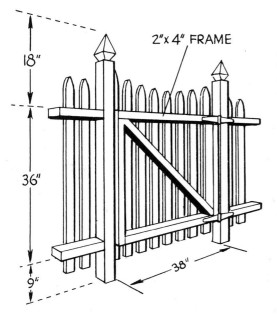

2" x 4" FRAME

18"

36"

9"

38"

Most gates can be built on the simple frame shown in both drawings. Be sure to use one diagonal brace to support weight, or as an alternative, wire and turnbuckle.

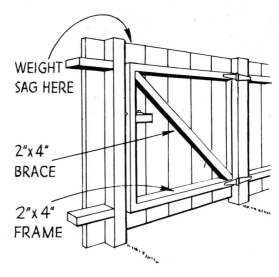

WEIGHT SAG HERE

2" x 4" BRACE

2" x 4" FRAME

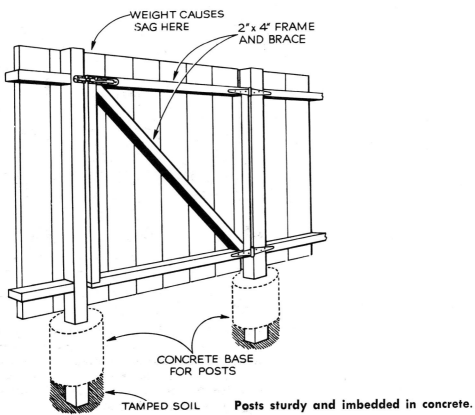

WEIGHT CAUSES SAG HERE

2" x 4" FRAME AND BRACE

CONCRETE BASE FOR POSTS

TAMPED SOIL   **Posts sturdy and imbedded in concrete.**

SEQUENCE FOR BUILDING A GATE

1
Plan for the gate as an integral part of the fence. Allow at least ½-inch space on sides so gate will swing easily. Set posts in concrete.

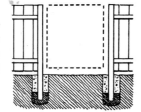

2
Build the frame of well-dried wood, preferably 2 x 4s. Use either of the joints shown. Use galvanized nails throughout to prevent rust and stains.

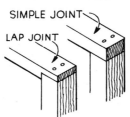

SIMPLE JOINT

LAP JOINT

3
Be sure to keep frame square.

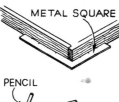

METAL SQUARE

4
After frame is nailed, measure diagonal brace. Use frame corner for marking, and angles will be correct. Saw these to leave pencil marks for a tight fit.

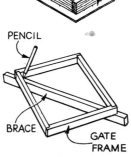

PENCIL

BRACE

GATE FRAME

5
One end of the cut diagonal, ready to insert.

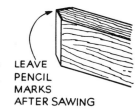

LEAVE PENCIL MARKS AFTER SAWING

6
Insert the diagonal and nail from two sides.

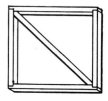

7
Attach hinges with noncorroding screws.

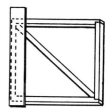

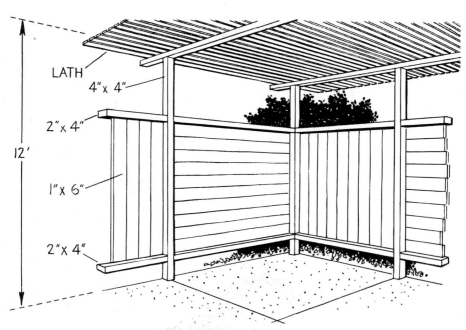

LATH

4" x 4"

2" x 4"

12'

1" x 6"

2" x 4"

Corner fence becomes a garden shelter. Extra-long posts support roof beams. Lath roofing provides part shade and coolness.

A picket fence made from old balusters and harmonizing with the details and the lines of the house. It enhances both the privacy and the feeling of space. Western Wood Products photo

A rustic cedar fence well scaled and textured to the environment. Deane Homes, Thousand Oaks, Calif.

A closer view of the same fence. It reaches above eye level to insure privacy, yet is low enough for its extent and situation not to affect the sense of ample space.

Fence and grounds should work well together. Dense planting to screen out city buildings and simple surface of fence create a feeling of serenity. Sea World

Shingles provide a decorative pattern and contrast handsomely with plantings and low rock wall. Garden of Mr. and Mrs. Arthur J. Priestly

Two lots fenced off only where privacy is desired, close to the houses. Foreground area left open to increase the feeling of space and view. Garden of Mr. and Mrs. Arthur J. Priestly

Slat fences that can work as louvers to reduce the effects of wind are good-looking and easy to build. Narrow spacing provides a good measure of privacy. Theodore Osmundson and Associates, L.A.

A section of fence built to make a place of shade. Decorative panels were added to break the broad expanse. Lloyd Bond, L.A.

The so-called board-on-board or shadow fence is said to have begun in Japan. It helps control wind, as a louver fence can, and at less cost. Braemar Homes. Armstrong and Sharfman, L.A.

Interesting and functional pattern of 2 x 4s set on edge, plus full boards to insure privacy and open areas for ventilation. Marc Askew, designer

A rather monotonous basket-weave fence is given excitement with a new panel of bamboo. Planting and lantern add to the effect. Hilda Wiedmann, designer

Square fence slats turned on edge. Pleasing light-and-shadow effect, especially in conjunction with slatted sun table. Marc Askew, designer

126

A slatted fence well chosen for simple Japanese type of design and planting. Strybing Arboretum

A grape-stake fence provides a foil for a concrete planting bed and also gives privacy. Braemar Homes. Armstrong and Sharfman, L.A.

Designed to mark the line between two areas, this fence acquires character simply by alternating full-length and short 2 x 4s. Sea World

Sturdy and natural-looking, creating a shifting play of light and shade throughout the day. Los Angeles County Arboretum

Lath nailed in an interesting pattern between upright 4 x 4s. Los Angeles County Arboretum

A simple slatted fence with cut 4 x 4 blocks as spacers. The alternating pattern adds a feeling of depth. Los Angeles County Arboretum

Basket weave, normally horizontal, is here adapted to a vertical design, broken in the center with three glass panels. Marc Askew, designer

Bamboo must be used simply when combined with other materials.

A simple panel fence showing typical construction. 2 x 4 is used on the bottom and 2 x 6 on top to tie the uprights together. Marc Askew, designer

A simple slatted fence designed to control wind and mark the end of an area. Theodore Osmundson and Associates, L.A.

A long fence is cut into sections and stepped one behind another, allowing room for planting and bringing renewed interest. Braemar Homes. Armstrong and Sharfman, L.A.

Excellent proportions and restraint combine for a distinguished design. Built of cypress, the fence is decay- and borer-resistant. Courtesy of Mr. and Mrs. George Mangan

Frame is made of 6 x 6s and 2 x 4s with panels faced inward. The effect is one of exciting depth. Wood is stained a dark gray tone, which adds to the effect. Golden Gate Center

A fence of wire that preserves the feeling of space yet provides security as well as design. Theodore Osmundson and Associates, L.A.

A purely Japanese treatment—board-on-board construction at the bottom and a white panel as contrast above. Strybing Aboretum

(Left) A good modern method of securing fenceposts is to bolt them above ground to two iron straps set in concrete. (Right) The finished result. Golden Gate Center. Lawrence Halprin and Associates, L.A.

Today's rail fence descended from pioneer days. This zigzag is but one of several possible patterns. Generally, 16-penny nails are needed to secure timbers, but not needed when wood is really heavy.

The triangle post fence. Peeled logs, 4 x 4s, or thicker timbers can be used.

Open-patterned concrete block can create delightful fences. La Posada Inn

Interesting effects can be created with open tile. This construction gives the effect of broken shade. Ciudad Obregon, Mexico

A gate set back in a shaded path has open slats to offer visibility from within and a feeling of space.

A gate that matches the fencing with latch set back. The design is most effective, the construction simple and easy. Theodore Osmundson and Associates, L.A.

An open gate with heavy ironwork in scale with its size. Strybing Arboretum

The principal cause of gate failure is inadequate hinging. Here three heavy strap hinges are minimal. Strybing Arboretum

Gates generally appear best when they match fencing. This one gains distinction by skipping top and bottom rails. Residence of Mr. and Mrs. George Mangan

A suggestion of Spain in turned-wood dowels between plain panels. This gate can be locked as well. Garden of Mr. and Mrs. Harold Hecht

A gate to a private beach. Diagonal strap increases strength. Every gate exposed to rough weather should be similarly constructed. La Posada Inn

With this type hinge, a gate can be lifted free without removing the hinge.

A selection of inexpensive gate latches: Top to bottom: a ring latch, a self-locking latch, a lockable hasp, and a top latch commonly used on a gate top.

When posts are buried they should be sunk 2 to 4 feet. Concrete poured around post adds to durability, but is not essential.

Use 4 x 4 or 6 x 6 (as here) for uprights. Mark point of sawing with a square to insure a perfect cut.

Dig posthole, then insert post and check for level on two of the four sides.

To secure posts until concrete is poured at the base, place a bottom support (in this case a 2 x 4) and nail post to it. Wood will help hold the post plumb until concrete hardens. (Here we are building a fence and a small paved patio.)

A close-up of the way in which fence posts are aligned and secured. Lines on 2 x 4 show lateral position, and nail holds post plumb.

After concrete has set, rails are cut and inserted between uprights. Use a block to force a tight fit. Toenail on two or four sides.

(Left) Cut panels to size, then nail. Use galvanized nails to avoid rust marks. (Right) Nail panels at bottom and top, then add trim—in this case a 1 x 2.

The finished project, a fence and display stand designed to hide a small utility structure behind.

7

Walls

Usually when I start to talk about the construction of walls, somebody in the audience raises his hand and asks, "What do *you* mean by 'walls'?"

In many sections of this country only masonry structures qualify as walls. Wooden structures have other names. Free-standing, they are fences. Against slopes, they are bulkheads. The walls discussed in this chapter may be made of wood, of concrete, of brick, or stones. They differ from fences primarily in being more solid.

What Kind of Wall?

In choosing which material may be best, consider its suitability for the purpose, the effect that you want, and the cost. For example, wood is excellent in modern and traditional settings, ideal for low retaining walls, and easy to work with and to assemble, reducing construction time. However, wood deteriorates faster in regions of low winter temperatures and considerable rain. For such a location, wood should be of greater strength than is needed in milder and drier places. Posts should be one size larger than for comparable fencing, and planks should be 2 inches thick.

Concrete blocks look well with many contemporary houses. Some people reject them as "cold" or "commercial"—and indeed they are often used without a touch of character—but actually their variety of shapes and textures makes them capable of warm and interesting effects. The largest blocks are 8 x 8 x 16 inches and sell for about fifty cents, providing great economics in time and cost. Although bricks are smaller, their uniform shapes and sizes also minimize construction time. Bricks are unexcelled for dignified, traditional styling, but are also good in modern schemes, especially when contrasted with wood, cement, or gravel. Adobe is another material most easy to work with, usually limited to informal treatment because of its rustic appearance, and limited also to drier climates (though it can take *some* rain well).

Stone walls are now a popular choice for many gardens. The irregularity of sizes and shapes of stones will increase construction time. Stone cut professionally and transported some distance can be quite expensive, but stone collected locally is usually much less so.

Poured concrete is the most versatile of wall materials, adaptable to styles as varied as colonial and Japanese. The construction methods for concrete offer design advantages: Walls can easily be curved or angled, surfaced smooth or rough, and decorated with embossed or inlaid designs. Total expense includes the complexity and sizes of forms, the amount of concrete needed, and its source. If you mix at home, costs can be reduced, but savings must be balanced against the mixing time.

Wooden walls

Post-and-plank retaining walls are handsome and easy to build. You erect them as fencing but with posts closer—every 4 to 5 feet—and sunk deeper—2½ to 3 feet. Planks should be secured to the uprights with galvanized bolts, which are designed for use in all woods. Select insect-and-moisture-resistant woods (heart redwood, cedar, or cypress), and apply preservatives liberally. Creosote is still good, but the newer chemicals are preferred by most builders.

Rugged, durable walls can be made of railroad ties or 4 x 4 and 6 x 6 timbers, which resemble them. The timbers can be aligned vertically or staggered and offset with pockets for planting. Either type of construction is easy. Begin with a foundation row of timbers. Excavate the soil to a depth equal to at least the width of the timbers; on this solid, leveled base, lay the foundation row. A concrete footing is not essential although desirable. When the first timbers are laid, add right-angle holding ties, called "dead-men." These are set from the facing timbers into slots excavated in the slope. Dead-men should be included every two or three rows. When all timbers are assembled, they are secured with a ½-inch steel rod driven through ⅜-inch holes drilled in the wood.

Dry stone walls

Low walls can be built of dry rock without mortar. Where the stones are available on the site, this kind of construction can be the least expensive of all. Free-standing dry walls need regular maintenance; dry walls against a slope can last for years, the natural drainage flowing between the stones often improving and settling the bulwark.

Place larger stones at the base, since a dry wall is only as reliable as its footing. Be sure they are sunk 12 to 18 inches below ground level in a smooth, even trench. Concrete is not required, but it can be used to increase durability. Slightly indent succeeding rows so that the face of the wall slants inward, the top offset 6 to 12 inches. Each stone should be tilted gently to the rear to resist ground pressures.

Fill in soil behind the stones as they are laid, tamping each layer with a 2 x 4 to fill unnoticed voids. At the end of each tier, moisten the soil well and tamp again. If the wall is to be planted, it is advisable to have any large-rooted plants in readiness and to insert them carefully as you proceed. The downward tilt of each layer of stone will direct rainwater to the plants; the roots should, of course, reach to the backing soil. Include a mixture of topsoil, manure, and humus in the planting area.

Cemented stone walls

The choice of stone depends on both the size of the wall and the climate. Shale, limestone, and sandstone should be restricted to occasional, low, lightweight walls. These materials absorb moisture easily and can freeze, split, and chip. When strength, height, and moisture-resistance are important, insist on tough rocks such as basalt and granite. Assemble all materials before building. Clean the pieces well, decide where the larger ones will go, and move them fairly near to their final positions. If the rocks have been washed, let them dry before adding mortar.

A good mortar formula is: 1 part fireclay, 2 parts cement, and 6 parts sand. Do not use hydrated lime, which is substituted for fireclay in some formulas, since lime may discolor stone. Mix the mortar in small batches to avoid premature drying. Combine the dry ingredients with a hoe, then add water until the mixture is slippery enough to slide from the blade. There is no way to estimate the amount of mortar required for a stone wall because of the irregular size of the joints and the unexpected gaps that must be filled. As much as a third of a wall may be mortar.

Blocks, bricks, adobe

Concrete blocks are available in two types: conventional, smooth-surfaced, and those containing cinder or pumice. The conventional type is heaviest (about 50 pounds), strongest, and water-resistant, ideal for general construction, foundations, and retaining and bearing walls.

Pumice block is lighter (about 26 pounds), can be nailed, drilled, and cut easily, and is excellent when neither strength nor moisture-resistance is as important as reduced weight. Both types are sold in full size, half size, and quarter size. Most often used for walls are these three: standard (8 x 8 x 16 inches), half (4 x 8 x 16), and corner (8-inch cube).

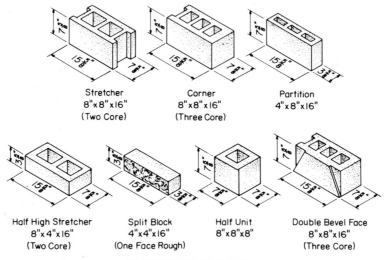

Stretcher
8"x8"x16"
(Two Core)

Corner
8"x8"x16"
(Three Core)

Partition
4"x8"x16"

Half High Stretcher
8"x4"x16"
(Two Core)

Split Block
4"x4"x16"
(One Face Rough)

Half Unit
8"x8"x8"

Double Bevel Face
8"x8"x16"
(Three Core)

CONCRETE BLOCKS
The seven most common sizes.
(Courtesy of Portland Cement Association)

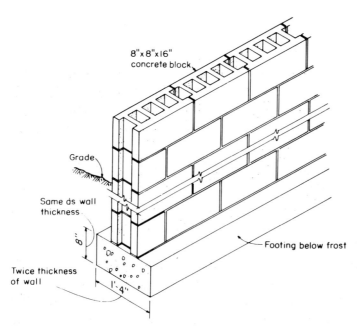

8"x8"x16"
concrete block

Grade

Same as wall
thickness

8"

Twice thickness
of wall

1'-4"

Footing below frost

FOOTING FOR 8-INCH-WIDE WALL When building a wall of concrete blocks the footing is important. It should be twice the thickness of the wall material and as high as the blocks used. The poured concrete should be placed below the frost line with room for at least one layer of concrete blocks below ground level.

(Courtesy of Portland Cement Association)

Procedure is the same for brick walls. Even the mortar can be the same. Each professional has his favorite formula. Mine is the Uniform Building Code Type B Mixture: 1 part fireclay or hydrated lime, 2 parts portland cement, and 9 parts mortar sand. (The warning against the use of lime does not apply here, since there is no staining danger with concrete.) Either fireclay or lime improves the viscosity of the mix. If you can't find the special mortar sand, substitute a 1-to-1 combination of plaster and concrete sand.

Clean the footing and apply the mortar, one block or brick at a time. Check each course with a level and a string laid across the face of the projected wall. If drainage is required, holes can be drilled through the blocks, or tubes can be set into the mortar.

Low brick walls can be the width of a single brick (4 inches) but walls more than 3 feet high should be 8 inches wide. Begin with corners, since they are used to align the face, then stretch a mason's line across the work. You can secure the line with nails driven into the fresh mortar or with special corner clamps.

The width of joints can be varied. Most professionals consider ½ inch best and claim that wide seams weaken a wall. Appearance is improved when joints are dressed, i.e., smoothed before they harden. The job can be done with a trowel tip or professional jointing tool. A section of ¾-inch pipe will dress a ½-inch seam quickly. Let the concrete harden for two weeks, then remove stains and efflorescence.

Adobe walls are erected similarly, and perhaps more rapidly, as a unit of adobe is approximately one and a half times the size of a standard brick.

Poured concrete

Forms must be built to support concrete until it hardens, and the success of a poured wall depends on the accuracy of the forms. You can make them of ½-inch or thicker plywood or of any inexpensive lumber that is at least 1 inch thick. A semigrooved material called shiplap is inexpensive and serviceable. Make sure, however, that whatever wood you choose is free of loose knots. One-inch pipe can be driven into the ground to support forms for low curbing. For most forms 2 x 4s on close centers are better. A wall that is not well supported can buckle as you pour. Curved sections may be formed with thin plywood, sheet metal, or "kerfed" wood.

When concrete is not to be painted, forms can be greased with a light oil to make them easier to remove. For a rough texture, use rough boards. For a rustic texture, place thin flat stones against the side of the form as you pour the mix. The stones will bond to the concrete and be exposed. For a smooth surface, work the mixture with a shovel, moving the blade up and down like a plunger near the edges, to force larger rocks to the center. Do not pour concrete when temperatures are likely to reach freezing before the mixture hardens. Frozen cement has little strength. The best formula for wall construction is the one suggested for walks (see under "Concrete," Chapter 5).

Drainage

A retaining wall is not a dam. The most common cause of failure is inability to withstand the build-up of water pressure. In places where moisture does not greatly accumulate, weep holes will do the job. They can be from ½ to 1 inch in diameter, set through the wall from the ground behind and slanted to the front. Gravel between the hole and the soil prevents clogging. On low walls the holes can be at 6-foot intervals, but in walls more than 4 feet high they should be inserted every 3 or 4 feet. If the flow of water is substantial, a gutter in front will prevent undercutting.

As the flow of water increases, drainage may be required in the slope—generally short sections of drain tile set low in the ground parallel with the wall. The tiles are separated an inch or so to improve the penetration of moisture, and the top is covered with tar paper to prevent clogging. Spread a layer of gravel above the paper to filter the soil. The tiles should carry the water beyond the wall. In severe cases diversion ditches may be required aboveground.

The buried side of masonry walls should be waterproofed. A common practice is to use asphaltic waterproofing, applied as you would paint. The material is recommended, but a new product is also worth considering: a colloidal clay called Bentonite. I have tried a product called Volclay (American Colloid Company), and I find it easy to use. Volclay is sold in 4-foot squares, with a kraft-paper backing making it easy to handle. The sheets are secured to the concrete with mastic, staples, or nails. Volclay is also available in powder that can be sprinkled before a footing is poured to minimize seepage.

Adding reinforcement

Many concrete walls less than 3 feet high can be made without reinforcing. Higher ones will need the support of steel bars set horizontally and vertically in the mix. Three-eighth-inch bars are satisfactory for footings; ½-inch rod is better for higher structures. When rods tie a wall to the footing, the reinforcing steel can be set 6 inches into the foundation at 4-foot intervals. In concrete-block construction the blocks are set over the horizontal rods, with mortar added at these places. When a wall exceeds rod height, set additional bars in the same holes to maintain alignment. The reinforcement should be carried to within 2 inches of the top.

Extra strength can be assured at the top of higher walls if bars are set horizontally around the top in the final few inches. On poured-concrete walls, bars are added as the mix reaches higher. For concrete-block structures, special U-shaped lintel blocks allow the same general procedure, the bars set in the U channel. At corners the rods should be bent to insure wrap-around strength. In the same way, bearing walls should be reinforced for at least 8 inches.

Building permits

These are generally required for all walls. Permissible heights and setbacks are defined in local codes. In many areas the height is the same as for fencing, but in some areas, masonry walls can be higher. There may be special restrictions on retaining and load-bearing walls. In some communities, masonry walls more than 4 feet high must be designed and supervised by a licensed engineer. Since the requirements vary, you must find out exactly what you may and may not attempt to do.

Chart VII   Materials for Masonry Walls

```
                              Concrete—one form only
                    Pourable
Material
                    Precut                      Brick and block
                              Regular
                              Irregular
                                              Stone and rock
```

The choice of materials for masonry walls is strangely divisible by two, as shown above. Stone and rock are also available in two forms: ashlar and rubble. Ashlar stone is long and narrow—fieldstone and slate are examples. Rubble is uncut, oddly shaped, and fitted to a wall like the pieces of a puzzle.

Chart VIII   Building the Foundation

Garden walls are only as reliable as their foundations, and with the possible exception of dry stone and low wooden walls, concrete foundations are required. Observe these four rules:

1. Excavation

Keep the trench square and level, as close to the foundation size as possible to avoid the need for forms. Keep to solid ground: never build a foundation on fill when other choices are available.

2. Light foundations

The footing should be at least 12 inches wide and 10 inches deep. In colder areas keep the concrete below the frost line—6 to 12 inches generally. If reinforcing rods are required, add as you pour.

3. Heavy foundations

Depth is commonly one-quarter the wall height. Width is approximately one-tenth the wall height. Reinforcing rods are essential.

4. Concrete

Use a standard mix. Level the top and allow to harden for two or three days. Clean the surface, then add mortar.

Chart IX   Painting Concrete

Concrete blocks can be allowed to weather naturally, but when a really waterproof surface is wanted, rely on cement paint. This type of paint can be applied in semisun; most brands will dry better in shade. In general, do not apply paints when temperatures are below 40° F. and do not paint a new block wall until it has set for at least twenty-four hours. Mix all paints in accordance with manufacturer's instructions.

1. Preparation   Remove whitish salt deposits, called efflorescence, with a mixture of 9 parts water and 1 part of muriatic acid. Rinse well.

2. Wetting   Dampen the blocks thoroughly until surface water is no longer visible. Fill small cracks with a paste made of the paint.

3. First coat   Use a coarse-bristled brush. Start with the joints, paint thoroughly, then move to the blocks. Keep the surface moist for twenty-four hours.

4. Second coat   Apply a second coat in the same manner. This application should be kept moist for two full days.

Chart X   How to Lay a Mortar and Stone Wall

1. Foundation   See Chart VIII, "Building the Foundation."

2. Base   Vary the size of rocks throughout the wall, but use a greater number of large rocks in lower levels to ensure strength.

3. Main section   Lay stones in natural positions just as they might lie on the ground. Rarely set rocks in positions that seem to defy gravity. Exceptions are modern walls of fieldstone, which can be set on end for decorative purposes.

4. Relationships Avoid pairing rocks of great difference in size. A strong wall needs a "bonded" construction, i.e., an overlapping of shapes and sizes.

5. Design   The best wall is one in which rocks are matched on the basis of size, shape, color, and texture, varied only enough to provide interest and strength.

6. Mortar joints Keep joints as thin as possible. It is the interlocking of rocks, rather than mortar, that achieves strength. Avoid continuous seams that follow from rock to rock in a regular pattern. The "lightning bolt" joint that works along several rocks can destroy a feeling of strength. When large voids must be filled, combine chips of stone with the mortar.

7. Finishing   If you want to smooth the seams, do so before the mortar hardens. Use a conventional jointing tool or a piece of thin pipe or tubing. Brush excess mortar away as you work. Persistent stains can be cleaned later with a mixture of water and muriatic acid.

A low retaining wall of wood, called a bulkhead in some localities. Marc Askew, designer

Wood is an excellent material for walls in dry and fairly mild climates. Marc Askew, designer

A low wall, with boards placed vertically, makes a pleasing foil for a heavily foliaged slope. Eckbo, Dean, Austin and Williams, L.A.

This handsome wall reverses the normal construction; it has the planking inside and the structure out. The wall slopes inward for both design and added strength. Heavy lag bolts hold the top rail in place.

Logs effectively retain a sandy slope on San Francisco Bay. Sunk several feet into the ground, they are secured with concrete. Theodore Osmundson and Associates, L.A.

Slopes can be held with low, stepped risers. These were made of poured concrete. They can be made from prefabricated concrete sections. Lytton Center

Timbers can be laid to hold gentle slopes. In most cases they will not need reinforcement; when they do, drill holes and drive pipe through. Eckbo, Dean, Austin and Williams, L.A.

Simple slopes can be held with logs laid against the hillside. Shorter logs ("dead-men") set into the hill anchor the retaining pieces. Theodore Osmundson and Associates, L.A.

Rugged, durable walls can be made of railroad ties or of timbers that resemble them. Various patterns can be created by using the wood in imaginative ways. Here the corners are exposed, the ends stepped to fit the slope.

Dead-men, at right angles to the wall timbers, are extended into the slope and will help to hold against pressures. Here dead-men are exposed but will be covered as soil is shoveled against the wall.

Beginning construction of a cedar post-and-plank wall. The 2 x 12 planks are treated on the side toward the soil with a preservative. In this case creosote is used because the stain will not show.

Posts are set as explained in Chapter 6, then planks are placed (in this case behind the posts), and leveled. They must be perfectly aligned to preserve the visual harmony of the structure.

Boltholes are drilled through post-and-cedar plank; ⅜ or ½ inch is generally recommended.

Bolts are inserted from the front so that the heads show (it is prettier), then bolt and lock washers are applied from the back and tightened. Use galvanized bolts to prevent rust.

Dry stone wall is aligned with string. Larger stones are set in a trench 1 to 2 feet deep. Sizes should be selected carefully.

Large rocks are set deep in the trench in a stable position. Robert Voris, builder

Soil is added behind the rocks, then tamped.

Tamped soil is further compacted with water. This procedure removes all pockets and ensures a durable foundation course.

150

A masonry stone wall, showing the way in which rocks are carefully fitted. For strength, sizes are lapped as brick would be.

Another stone wall with masonry. The seams are narrow, since strength comes from the rock, not the masonry.

A beautifully fitted stone wall with each piece cut for its place. Strength is gained from the positioning of the rocks and not from masonry.

Natural rocks can be inserted into stone walls to break the line and add interest. Garden of Mr. and Mrs. Arthur J. Priestly

A dry wall fitted relatively loosely and yet carefully for strength. Changes in sizes of rocks add to interest. Strybing Arboretum, Thomas D. Church, L.A.

A low stone wall marks the property line and repeats stones used in the background.

A low rock wall holds a short bank and provides a raised planting bed.

A low curbing gives a feeling of security and a warning as the property line ends and deep water begins. Three photos of garden of Mr. and Mrs. Arthur J. Priestly

Lava rock is cut precisely to fit, with the result a tight, solid wall that requires a minimum of masonry.

(Left) A rough rock retaining wall and curbing, in handsome contrast with the simple formality of house and upper level. (Right) Detail of the same wall, with perfectly handled terrazzo stairs. Garden of Mr. and Mrs. Montgomery Fisher

A low stone wall marks the end of a property and supports face of slope beyond.
Garden of Mr. and Mrs. George Mangan

(Left) A single layer of bricks defines a planting area. It is laid on a shallow pad of
poured concrete. The left foreground area will be filled with earth, then planted with
grass. Mayfair Homes. (Right) A low brick wall separates lawn from sunken patio with
a fine simplicity. Deane Homes

Fieldstone wall creates a dramatic area for planting. Mayfair Homes

A low fieldstone wall retains a slope beside a pool. Braemar Homes

Adobelike concrete blocks make an attractive low-walled planter. The top is edged with concrete for a finished appearance. Mayfair Homes

Raised curbing provides a shallow ledge for sitting and offers planting places for trees. A distinguished contrast of materials. Eriksson, Peters & Thoms, L.A.

Conventional concrete blocks are the heaviest, strongest, and most water-resistant, generally recommended for wall construction. Alignment creates an interesting pattern. Reinforcement inside blocks gives durability. Garden of Mr. and Mrs. William Robinson

A square pylon is created from adobe to support a dramatic lantern at an entrance.
Marc Askew, designer

A wall of broken concrete is set dry and tapered slightly to increase stability. On a poured-concrete platform this wall is quite durable. Eriksson, Peters & Thoms, L.A.

An imaginative rock wall in Mexico. Small rocks are set in concrete. White boat is designed with shells.

A low concrete retaining wall decorated with rock set deep into it, then emphasized with the concrete cut back. Los Angeles County Arboretum

8

Constructing
and Furnishing Patios

The patio is an important aspect of today's life-style; if you don't have one, do consider building one yourself. It need be neither costly nor complex. To plan a successful patio, begin with three general considerations: the weather and exposure, the expected flow of traffic, and the design in relation to the patio's chief purpose —a small intimate one for family enjoyment or a large patio for entertaining.

Weather first

You have seen patios that ignore the climate. Some are cold and windy, others hot and dry, many uncomfortable and often untenable. Landscape architects maintain that the pleasure we get from an area relates directly to the way it meets and "controls" the weather, and they are right. The best patios I know are planned to exploit either the sun or the shade.

Sun-inviting patios face south or west and are excellent in cool regions where the sun's rays are welcome the year round. A southern exposure is warmest, inviting the full day's sun, drying quickly after rains, and warming fastest on winter days. A western exposure offers greater contrast: coolness in the morning and warmth in the afternoon. Neither location is suggested for hot parts of the country, the South and Southwest. There, sun-facing patios generally need some areas of extensive shade, and planting to screen or filter the slanting rays of late afternoon sun.

Shade-inviting patios face north or east and are recommended for warm states. They are cool, restful, and even a little moist. A northern exposure is coolest. Sections of a patio close to a north wall may never

159

see the sun. An eastern outlook welcomes the cooler morning sun and wards off hot evening rays. In cold climates, such patios may require auxiliary heating and may never dry in winter.

Often compound patio shapes can make effective use of both sun and shade. My own house has an L-shaped area that faces west and north. Some houses, especially those with east and west wings, have one patio facing south for winter use and another to the east or north for summer.

Traffic patterns and privacy

The second consideration in locating the patio is the floor plan of the house. In the summer, traffic should flow in and out naturally without disturbance. A patio makes a house seem larger and brighter.

The backyard is the most obvious place, normally having the greatest space and privacy. But if traffic flow suggests other areas, almost any part of the yard can work. A front patio can be created with fencing, but it will surely have less privacy, greater noise, and interruptions. Fencing high enough to hide house lines is prohibited in some areas, and when allowed, is costly, because the workmanship, constantly on view, must be of fine quality. The suitability of side yards depends upon space. Most are narrow and confining and, because setback distances are limited, less private. But a patio there does make use of space normally wasted.

Wherever you build, traffic should flow from the garden to the patio as naturally as from the house to the patio. The pattern is controlled by three factors: the location of entries (doors, gates, and paths), important centers (cooking, conversation, or play), and furniture. Keep cooking centers away from central areas, and route traffic around activities and conversation areas. A child's play area should be removed from the main patio, perhaps separated by a low fence, and garden work centers should be similarly detached. Build service centers not only for laundry and garden uses but for storage as well. Convenient furniture racks keep a patio uncluttered.

Create privacy with gratings, screens, and fences. Use overhead structures to block a low terrace from higher neighboring ones. Build one as you would a lightweight deck, with a grid of 1 x 4 or 1 x 6 lumber. Tie it to the house on one side and to 4 x 4 posts on the other. If timbers are set close you may not need cover. If a further cover is required, use fabric or translucent plastic. Canvas is traditional. Burlap is neither colorful nor as durable as canvas, but offers improved ventilation through an open weave. At eye level, build fencing and relieve the structure with borders of thick, tall shrubs.

Wind can be subdued by paneled fences that divert gusts or by louvers and screens that reduce their force. Various ways of mitigating wind are discussed in Chapter 6. Use solid panels for privacy, cutouts and embossed patterns for decoration, and glass to preserve or dramatize a view.

Size for proper scale

From the standpoint of landscape design, the best patios are in scale with the lot, house, and the recreations they support. Inside a room, every detail is related to the enclosing walls and ceiling, but amid trees and open space, patio and furniture groupings must be larger just to compete. For example, only a big area can hold its own surrounded by hills. Yet you may not want to sacrifice too many trees or masses of shrubs simply to make the patio larger. In that case, plan the patio as a unit with some salient planting, tying it into your landscape, or else keep it close to the house, harmonizing with the house as much as possible. If there is one rule for size, it might be this: Let your patio be larger than the largest room in your house.

Even a small place may require a 300-square-foot patio to accommodate a picnic table, barbecue, chaise lounge, and a few chairs. When space is limited, a few tricks help make the most of it. Begin by reducing the amount of furniture and the number of activities the patio is to offer. Fewer activities mean less congestion. Increase the center space with the built-in seats, cabinets, etc., on the perimeter. Curve the corners to break the sense of confinement. Avoid glaring colors. Pave with smaller brick, tile, or stone to accent size comparisons. Create variety with new levels, raised planters, and steps that lead the eye upward, increasing the illusion of space. When otherwise practical, keep fences low to carry the eye beyond the property line.

A poolside patio can be two patios in one: near the house, a quiet place for rest and conversation; near the pool, an open space for sunbathing. You may also want to include shade and a place to dress.

As size increases, keep the layout in scale. Place important areas, such as conversation and cooking centers, nearer the house to reduce steps. Break expanses of paving with variations in texture or squares of planting. If in planning, a large patio threatens to appear barren, try two smaller ones, or make a second one level with a pool. Steps should be wider and longer, and plantings larger and fuller.

At any size a patio, or any of its parts, must be perfectly level. When the ground is uneven there are three reasonable solutions: excavate high areas, fill low ones, or build part of the patio as a deck. If there is a substantial variation between ground and house levels, where should the patio be placed? The answer depends upon several factors. The greater the variation of topography near the house, the more one hesitates to place a patio there, and yet a ground-level location has a pleasant "close-to-the-soil" feeling that no deck can convey.

If the space for the patio is only a few feet lower than the house, you can break the descent by a rather generous platform at the door. Wide, shallow steps will make access easy, comfortable, and inviting. When the distance is greater, you may prefer a split-level patio, the part closest to the house as a deck and the part farther away at ground level. And again, the connecting stairs should have extra-wide treads.

A choice of designs

When I was a child, patios were formal and informal. If formal, they were laid out with center lines and ovals strung together like beads. If informal, they had center lines and ovals broken by unrelated walks and curbings or an extravagant use of free curves. Now patio designs belong more freely to the landscape as a whole. There are three basic designs, which can be modified and adapted to each situation.

Rectangular designs are seldom wrong. Squares and oblongs are clearly related to the shapes of most houses and property divisions, most walks and drives. An acute angle is still considered "modern" by many people, but when space is limited, a patio set at a 90° angle seems to create a feeling of greater balance and repose.

Free-form shapes are in vogue because they are flexible and adaptable. When the size is in proportion to the house and when the lines conform to some degree with those of the garden, a free form can be exciting. As you plan an unconventional shape, begin with a rectangle, then soften the edges and proportions until the result seems pleasing. Avoid sharp corners (or many of them), and never pinch the lines and narrow areas until the form seems squeezed.

Circular designs are not common, but with imaginative planting can be fine in large areas. Often a circle is used within a rectangle, the paving changing in texture.

Try designing on paper first, then in your yard. Forms can be laid out full size with a garden hose to give you an idea of their feasibility. If you have serious doubts, consult a landscape architect. Professional advice is in the end a great saver of time, errors, and money.

2. THE RIGHT LOCATION? Place the patio in relation to the floor plan of your house. Traffic between should be direct and easy. Ready access from living room. Not too far from kitchen.

3. HOW BIG IS BIG ENOUGH? The scale out-of-doors is larger than within rooms. As a rule, a patio should be larger than the largest room in your house. Enough space for an unusual number of guests.

4. WHAT KIND OF SURFACING? No place for economy here. Choose from long-term materials—concrete, brick, pacing block, flagstone, and wood. Consider their relative strength, texture, maintenance, and repair.

5. HOW MUCH PRIVACY? Depends upon how sociable you are. If you entertain often, privacy will be less important than if you want the patio for reading and work. Screens, overhead grids, trees can create some measure of privacy.

6. WHAT KIND OF EQUIPMENT? Include recreational gear, tables for cards, and games. Fans for very warm areas, outdoor fireplace for cold ones. Cooking facilities add to the fun. If children do not have their own play area, include a sandbox, perhaps a slide.

Paving materials

Construction methods are the same as those used in laying walks and paths and are discussed in Chapter 5. Popular paving materials are briefly described below to give comparisons of cost, color, coverage, and durability.

1. TEMPORARY

MATERIALS	COLOR	COMMENTS
Pea gravel, ½ to 1″ diam.	White to gray	One of the least expensive materials. Easily applied and best when contained between wooden headers. Must be replenished often. Average coverage per ton: 100 square feet to 2″ depth.
Crushed brick, roofing gravel, ½ to 1½″ diam.	White, red, green, yellow	Similar coverage and characteristics. Like pea gravel, remains loose underfoot even after rolling.

2. SEMIPERMANENT
   MATERIALS   COLOR   COMMENTS

Red rock, decomposed granite, pulverized rock, ½ to 1″ diam.	Red-brown, brown, gray, varies according to region from which it comes	Relatively inexpensive, but some may be costly because of local shortage. Easily applied. Will pack hard after rolling but should be contained between headers. May wash with rains and must be replaced every two to three years. Coverage per ton: 100 square feet to 2″ depth.

3. PERMANENT
   MATERIALS

Brick of all types	Various tones of red and brown, yellow, white	Moderate to expensive, depending on type. Common brick and pavers are suggested. Easily applied, especially over sand or concrete. Must be properly laid to prevent deterioration.
Tile	Earthen, also in fired-in colors and patterns	Generally costly but smooth underfoot. Ideal for heavy usage, such as dancing. Tile is generally formal. Some grades will withstand frost; in northern areas check with your dealer.
Concrete	Naturally gray but can be colored with pigments	Plastic and flexible. Can be used to create any shape required. Extremely durable and only moderately expensive. A good depth is 4 inches. Never pour during freezing weather. Can be given various patterns and textures.
Flagstone	Gray but can be colored with pigments	Easily laid and best over sand or concrete base. Low maintenance. Coverage is dictated by the size of the slab plus a ½-inch joint.

PERMANENT MATERIALS	COLOR	COMMENTS
Wood	Natural or can be stained in natural shades	Can be laid as blocks or planking over sand as you would brick, or over timbers. Little glare and great resilience. Wood can become slippery and mossy in moist, shady areas; may crack in dry, hot ones. Insect-resistant woods recommended. Expensive finishes, from pecky to smooth.

Portable barbecues

GRILLE.   Should be large enough to cook food for the normal number of guests at one time. A movable grille gives maximum heat control. A stationary grille should be at least 6 inches above the fire.

GRATE.   Must be of cast-iron or heavy steel for durability. Should be removable for easy cleaning; a special lifting tool is handy. Inexpensive braziers may have no grate. For these, spread 2 or 3 inches of sand on bottom to prevent burning through the metal.

WEIGHT.   A heavy barbecue is generally better built than a light one, but be certain the added weight is not due to useless accessories. A portable unit is of little value if you can't move it easily. As weights increase, be sure wheels and axles are stronger.

ACCESSORIES.   Rotisserie, smoker, warming oven, and cutting board are all handy—if you cook outside often enough to warrant them. When the unit is equipped with an electric motor, be sure it is properly grounded. A three-prong plug is best.

Flowing line, simple plantings, fine brick pavement radiating from an old tree, create a feeling of complete naturalness. Deane Homes

North-facing patio, cool and restful in a climate of warm summers. Evergreens and unusual paving give permanent interest. Lloyd Bond, L.A.

(Left) A simple patio on the south side of a house in a cool climate where the sun's rays are always welcome. Strybing Arboretum. (Right) Expanding circles in brickwork make this small area seem larger. Variations in tones of brick harmonize with the shadows.

170

Paved areas should be scaled in relation to the lot and house, and continuity of design is important throughout. Residence of Mr. and Mrs. Irving Hammer

A series of paved areas variously shaped and edging a large open space invite movement.

Rough-finished concrete and stones tie together a patio, walk, and retaining wall.

A change of levels and textures increases interest greatly. Two long platforms lead to the steps and modify their rather abrupt feeling.

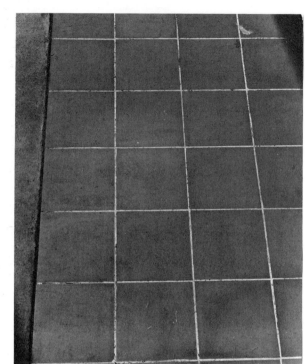

Wood is suitable patio material and can be laid over sand or concrete. Small planks and blocks are handled as brick. Surfaces from pecky to smooth are available.

Tile is a good choice for patio pavement, smooth underfoot and well adapted to formal styling.

Hexagonal concrete pavers have a pleasing combination of rustic texture and formal pattern. Rough surface and gray color minimize glare.

A fine example of materials contrasted: old cobble-stones salvaged from the streets of San Francisco, a band of aggregate concrete, and finally paver brick. Golden Gate Center. Lawrence Halprin and Associates, L.A.

An aggregate concrete surface offers good traction and a naturalistic appearance, fine in itself for informal patios and effective in juxtaposition to smooth textures.

Section of an interesting pattern: small tiles crossing through a mosaic of stones laid in concrete.

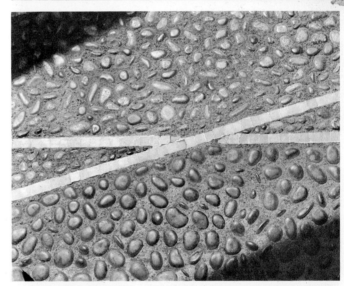

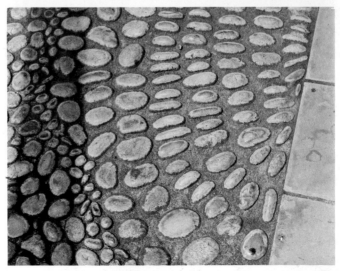

Rock can be used in random patterns or in a carefully controlled mosaic, as here. Mosaic is laid in wet concrete, then, when concrete is partly dry, it is washed to expose the surface.

Handmade tiles set in concrete provide a charming and unique design.

Strip of embossed tile between two kinds of aggregate.

A fire pit is excellent for both cooking and heating. The pit is lined with firebrick, and the fire built on stones. Residence of Mr. and Mrs. David Foster. Armstrong and Sharfman, L.A.

When not in use the pit is closed off by wooden covers.

An aboveground fire ring. It requires little space, can serve as a stove or a heater, and makes a gathering place. Theodore Osmundson and Associates, L.A.

Outdoor heating is a comfort in many country places. This gas heater is easy to install and economical. It warms a large area effectively. Braemar Homes. Armstrong and Sharfman, L.A.

A simple metal fireplace, having an efficient spark catcher on top. It can burn wood, pressed logs, or briquets.

A new idea in outdoor stoves—a permanently mounted gas barbecue.

9

Decks

A man in Salt Lake City defines a deck, with superb simplicity, as "a patio lifted off the ground." He makes equally clear the reasons for decking versus patio: "Differences in house and lot levels or excessive patio construction costs usually settle the issue." He was thinking of his own house on rolling land in the Wasatch Mountains. The living room is well above ground level and a patio would have required a series of steps. "It would have been awkward," he said, "and a deck was the only solution."

But there are other reasons. A man in Seattle wanted an outdoor entertaining center on a lot that sloped away from the rear of his house. There was space to make a small patio by excavation, but several factors kept him from doing this. Excavation estimates were high; a septic tank and drain field prohibited major concrete work; and the land was too attractively wooded to scar. Instead, he built a two-level deck that naturally descended the slope.

A man in Los Angeles built his house on a steep suburban lot. The front fell sharply from street to building site, and the foundation of the house rose 7 feet to return the main floor to street level. The area between street and house was useless until covered with decking.

Planning

The best decks are those so placed in relation to the house as to invite a free flow of traffic, but detached decks are practical in special situations, as where a certain location offers a fine view or unusual privacy. Choose the location carefully, on the basis of exposure to sun and wind, the plan of the property in general, and the particular functions the deck will serve. Before making a decision, observe the effects of the sun at different times. Chart the hours the first rays strike and the last leave, and the hours of greatest heat. Such a table will give an idea of the feasibility of an area and the controls required. Remember that the warm sides of a house are south and west, and the cool are north and east.

When differences between house and lot levels are slight and one or two steps of little concern, deck height can be flexible. At ground level a deck doubles for a patio and should be of patio dimensions. There construction is uncomplicated and size is seldom restricting. But as heights increase, the support system becomes more elaborate and may necessitate your "building small" to build at all. Then a deck of 150 to 200 square feet can seem generous. Normally, you build high to take advantage of a view or to increase house space, and low to keep a close connection with a garden or to ensure privacy.

Scale—a matter of height, surface size, and shape—is important. The supports, the flooring, and the seating must be in a practical and pleasing relationship with one another and with the house and garden. Start your planning with the deck area. When you have defined its shape, the supports can be designed to proper scale.

Auxiliary structures to reduce wind, increase shade, or create privacy can be similar to those used for patios. But consider carefully any side effects the control may produce. A screen that blocks wind may also block a view. Trees can function as screens when nearby and close together but may shut out air. Evergreen trees, even at a little distance, are good windbreaks; however they may, en masse, create a very somber effect. In regions where spring and autumn evenings are chilly, heating may be needed. The butane and electrical units suggested for patios will work well for decks.

Site preparation

Even though a deck is built aboveground, the ground itself will have to be cleared of most vegetation and graded or provided with drainage. Beneath high decks some vegetation can remain if there is no fire hazard, but for appearance and safety it is better removed. In some parts of the country where drought is apt to occur, undergrowth becomes a special summer fire danger, and decks may be prohibited. And we must admit that some men and women will always be careless about matches and cigarettes, that there is a tendency to throw things over railings. Most communities permit construction when certain specified conditions are met. In general these are:

1. A design to trap as little up-slope draft as possible. (A con-

ventional deck may function as a chimney, first drawing the on-rushing heated air, then attracting flames.)

2. The removal of brush for a distance of 30 feet in all directions. The growth may be replaced with grass, vines, or ground-cover plants.

3. Thinning the brush for 40 feet beyond the green belt; again replacing with grass or low shrubs where practical. If soil must be held, native grasses can be used.

Regrowth may be inhibited simply by lack of sunlight beneath a low deck, but in most instances controls are needed. The least expensive is a layer of plastic sheeting or building paper. Either can be laid over growing weeds, but functions better over cleared ground. Sheets can be secured with heavy stones and camouflaged with layers of gravel.

In the early stages of growth, weeds are easily removed by hoe and steel rake. For weeds that have developed tough stems and deep roots, you will probably need some proprietary weed-killer. There are a number of these on the market. Read directions carefully. Remember that most chemical solutions are dangerous and each should be considered for its advantages and drawbacks. Some weed-killers sterilize the soil, kill plant life, then leach away in weeks. But others are almost permanent, like sodium arsenate, which is highly toxic. Rock salt is effective although slower acting.

Minor grading may be required to lower a hump, reduce part of a slope, or prepare small areas for footings. Much of the earth-moving can be done by hand with shovel and wheelbarrow, but if large areas are involved, machines will probably be needed. Bulldozers, skip loaders, and tractors are charged for by the hour ($12 to $50), plus transportation, but their speed when well operated makes them a worthwhile investment.

Where erosion is threatened on sloping land, the best prevention is soil-binding plants that can be kept from invading the ground directly under a deck but allowed to multiply and spread rapidly on adjacent areas—provided there is no conflict with local fire-control regulations. An outstanding bank stabilizer is the perennial crown vetch (*Coronilla varia*). Japanese honeysuckle, the memorial rose (*Rosa wichuraiana*), and the various prostrate junipers and cotoneasters are also excellent. On small slopes, in shade, pachysandra, ajuga, and English ivy will hold the soil. In sunny places, the perennial candy tuft (*Iberis sempervirens*), creeping phlox (*Phlox subulata*), and various sedums will do the job.

To support a deck where soil is unstable because of conditions that cannot be corrected, as an earlier fill, very steep slope, or the possibility of earthquake, the pilings should be of steel and sunk to bedrock. Against a very strong building, a hanging platform can sometimes be cantilevered. Where this is feasible (and you will need a civil engineer's opinion), the hanging deck can be most attractive and airy.

On most lots drainage is a matter of channeling surface water to reduce erosion. The easiest solutions are a shallow ditch or a "French drain." The ditch can be little more than an earthen trough, although it is better when lined with concrete. A French drain is a deeper trench with a base of crushed rock, a line of drain tiles, and a covering of building paper and additional rock. The drain tiles should be separated slightly to allow water to seep into the soil. The building paper can be placed directly above the tile (not around it), or over a layer of gravel. The gravel is commonly exposed at the surface, but when a drain passes through a cultivated area, as a lawn, it can be sunk to include a cover of soil and grass.

Basic Construction

Footings

Decks can be made of various materials, as wood, steel, or concrete. Wood is the common choice, because it is inexpensive and easy to work with. Insect-resistant woods are not essential when footings are provided to keep the wood dry and aboveground. Then decks can be made with a range of softwoods, though resistant woods are often chosen for their texture and color.

Start construction with the footings that level and support the basic structure. Each upright has its own footing. Building codes usually prohibit the setting of posts in concrete because of the danger of decay and termite infestation. Instead, cast footings are used. For lower decks use precast pyramid blocks set on the soil, but for higher or heavier projects use footings cast in holes dug at the site. Depths are often defined by local building codes, commonly to solid soil or bedrock.

Upright posts can be anchored to footings in several ways. Precast blocks normally have a square of wood seated in the top, and blocks cast on the site can be similarly equipped. Posts are toenailed to the blocks on two or more sides. A better system is to cast a ½-inch rod (drift pin) vertically in each block. When a hole is drilled in the post, the post can be slipped over. Be sure to insert a small section of building paper or foil between wood and post to prevent the staining that results from wood-to-metal contact. A newer method features the metal fasteners shown in Chapter 6. One end of the fastener is embedded in concrete and the other, sized for the post, has predrilled nail holes. These galvanized fasteners are reliable and sturdy.

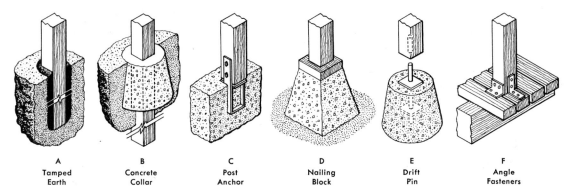

A Tamped Earth	B Concrete Collar	C Post Anchor	D Nailing Block	E Drift Pin	F Angle Fasteners

POST FOOTINGS

Six methods of mounting deck posts to the ground. The simplest is by setting directly in the ground, and for many structures tamped earth is satisfactory. But the other methods provide more rigidity and—in the case of posts above the ground line—more protection against rot, moisture, and insects. In all cases be sure to use a resistant wood.

(Courtesy of California Redwood Association)

Footing positions must be accurate and square. Assuming the structure is attached to your house, use the house as a starting point and rely on a carpenter's simple trick to guarantee a perfect square— the "rule of 3-4-5."

Fasten a carpenter's line to the house at the point at which the deck begins.

Extend the line out to the point at which it ends.

Measure along the line 4 feet from the house and make a mark.

Then measure along the house 3 feet from the line and make a mark.

Place a rule from the 3-foot mark on the house to the mark on the line. If the angle is perfectly square, the rule will measure 5 feet. If the measurement is off, adjust the line until its mark coincides with the 5-foot indication on the rule.

Finally, secure the string and position the footings.

Distance between footings is determined by the beams used above the uprights. A 4 x 4 beam can safely span 4 feet; a 4 x 6, 6 feet; and a 4 x 8, 8 feet. Place footings on these centers; i.e., the centers of the upright posts will be 4, 6, or 8 feet apart. Use the line to check for square in all directions. See the photographs of footings in Chapter 6.

Posts

The uprights can be of wood or of concrete. The usual choice is wood. Softwoods can be used with footings, and the softwood 4 x 4 is popular because an 8-foot length weighs less than 50 pounds yet supports 8,000 pounds. When loads are greater, as in snow country, or when a 4 x 4 seems visually inadequate, select heavier timbers from sizes 4 x 6 to 8 x 10. Your lumber company will advise you. A 4 x 6 will support 14,000 pounds, and an 8 x 10 more than 50,000 pounds.

Good supports can also be fabricated from pieces of smaller lumber, as 2 x 4s and 2 x 6s. The built-up post offers advantages of reduced weight and less chance of warping. The components can be joined with nails, screws, and bolts. If you use nails, choose at least a 20-penny size. Space the posts no more than 4 feet apart, and increase the security of each with bolts, top and bottom.

Peeled logs are another possibility. They are common in the West and available in other parts of the country. Sturdy and rustic-looking, they can often be legally buried in concrete. But log posts are heavy, not always straight, and their dimensions are uneven. One end may vary from another.

Post heights should be measured with care and timbers cut evenly to insure a level, stable deck. If the structure is to be attached to a house, start measurements there. Nail a ledger board or face plate— i.e., a supporting 2 x 4 strip—along the house the length of the deck. It should be placed at the height at which the joists, not the deck surface, will rest. In other words, it should be nailed below the final deck level as much as the combined thickness of decking and joists. Check the board for level before nailing. On a concrete wall, you can use a ledger strip or individual metal hangers. Both can be attached with special inserts.

Post height can be determined in two ways. From the ledger board measure the distance to house ground line. To that distance, add or subtract any difference between the footing height and the ground line. Or you can get the post height visually, as I prefer to do, because the chance for error is diminished. Set up a row of posts, leaving each slightly longer than required. Brace each temporarily, then run a level line from ledger to posts. Mark each and cut.

Concrete uprights are called piers. Their height is measured the same way (obviously before pouring and not after). They can be made from several forms. A 12-inch sewer pipe is good. It can be filled with cement and left intact. Other possibilities include a detachable rolled metal form and a preformed fiber tubing, which is removed like paper after the mix hardens. Use the concrete formula given in Chapter 5, and be sure to add reinforcing rods. Local codes may define both rod size and the number required.

Top elements

The beams are laid above the uprights and bear the heaviest load. Often they are the size of the uprights, to which they can be secured in several ways—by toenailing, by screws and bolts, or by the new metal fasteners, which are excellent and available in several types at most lumberyards.

A network of smaller lumber, called joists or stringers, is added at right angles to the beams. It strengthens the framework and makes possible shorter lengths of the decking that follows. Joists are generally placed on 16- to 24-inch centers to provide support for the flooring. They can be laid over the beams or set flush with them. If they are placed flush, fasten at the bottom either a 2 x 4 cleat or a metal hanger. Toenailing is not reliable.

The floor or surface of the deck is not a structural member and can be of smaller lumber. Common materials are 2 x 4s and 2 x 6s, although 2 x 3s and 1 x 4s are occasionally used. Redwood and cedar are good choices because they color well and resist checking and decay, but fir, pine, and other softwoods can be recommended. When you order lumber, specify exact lengths so that sawing will be reduced.

If the floor boards are to be laid parallel with the house, begin at the house; if boards are to be at right angles, start at one end. To ensure a perfect right angle, again apply the 3-4-5 rule. If there is to be space between boards, cut guide blocks of that width. They will make for perfect alignment. If possible, place the lumber, bark-side up, to reduce crazing, cupping, and checking. To determine the bark side, turn the lumber so that the growth rings, seen at the cut ends, reach their highest point at the top and circle downward.

Sometimes solid flooring is needed, as over a garage. Exterior plywood is fine for this. It may be painted or covered with tiles or outdoor carpeting. If there is danger of water pooling, be sure to place a drain at the lowest point. A little forethought in planning any solid-floor deck, as to ease of cleaning, sweeping, and hosing, may save work and inconvenience later on.

Railings

Building codes of many towns require a railing if decks are more than 3 or 4 feet aboveground. On some low decks a railing completes the design. If spaced on close centers (3 to 5 feet), 2 x 4 uprights are often strong enough to meet code requirements, but thicker materials may be visually better. When possible the uprights should be bolted to the deck beams.

The cross rail can be attached in several ways and take various forms. With a table or radial saw, you can make handsome tailored cuts, grooves, and dado strips.

The entire deck can be left unfinished or covered, as you might a fence, with paint, stain, or water seal. If you wish to keep a natural look, use a nonstaining preservative; if you want color, add a reliable stain plus a recommended protective coating. If you decide on paint, be sure to apply a good sealer as the first coat.

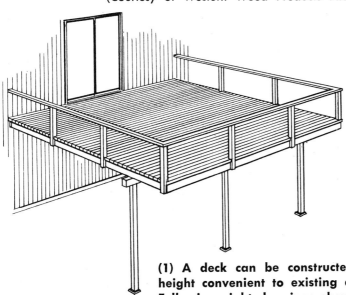

(1) A deck can be constructed at any reasonable height convenient to existing or possible entrances. Following eight drawings show how to build a 12-foot-square deck. Dimensions can be altered to fit your requirements.

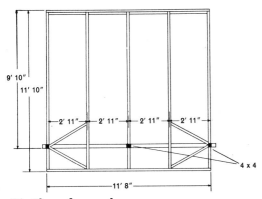

(2) Plan, from above.

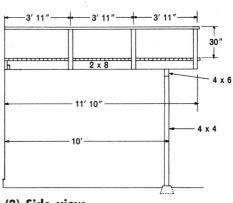

(3) Side view.

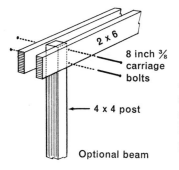

Optional beam

(4) Deck beams are erected on posts set on piers. Begin by digging to solid ground to install pier blocks, as shown in (7) on page 186. Beam can be a single 4 x 6, as shown in (7), or made of two 2 x 6s, as shown here. This is the optional approach.

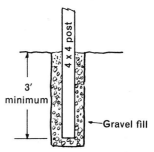

Optional foundation
(Posts may be heart cedar, or pressure treated)

(5) Another option. Posts should be set on piers if possible, but they can be placed in holes. Wood must be insect-resistant or specially treated.

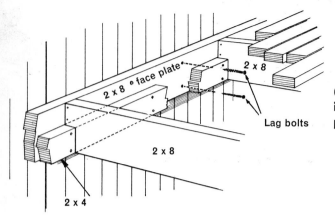

2 x 8 face plate
2 x 8
Lag bolts
2 x 8
2 x 4

(6) Notch the stringers and attach to the nailing plate, a 2 x 4 called a ribbon or base support. Check for plumb and level.

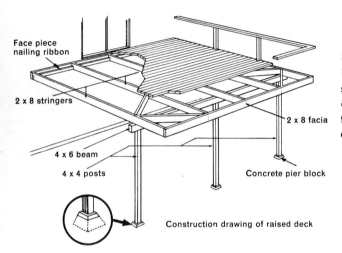

Face piece
nailing ribbon
2 x 8 stringers
2 x 8 facia
4 x 6 beam
4 x 4 posts
Concrete pier block

Construction drawing of raised deck

(7) After framework is built install decking. Use a block of wood or 10-penny nail for spacer between strips. Nail decking to stringers with 10-penny nails. Use galvanized nails to prevent rust and staining. Check alignment of boards frequently as you progress.

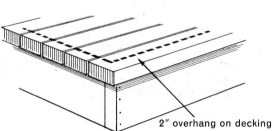

2" overhang on decking

(8) Allow a 2-inch overhang for appearance.

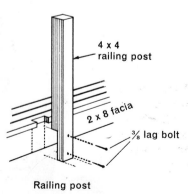

4 x 4
railing post
2 x 8 facia
⅜ lag bolt

Railing post

(9) Notch railing posts and decking, then predrill railing posts and stringers and facia, and attach. Use two ⅜ x 3-inch lag bolts for strength. Add the railing cap with two 10-penny nails.

MATERIAL LIST
FOR 12' x 12' DECK

Quantity	Dimension	Use	Length
1	2 x 8	Face Plate	12'
1	2 x 8	Facia	12'
5	2 x 8	Stringers	12'
4	2 x 8	Diagonal Braces	3' 3"
1	4 x 6	Beam	14'
3	4 x 4	Posts	Undetermined
1	2 x 4	Nailing Ribbon	12'
39	2 x 4	Decking	12'
8	4 x 4	Railing Posts	4'
3	2 x 4	Railing Cap	14'

3 Concrete Pier Blocks

5 Gallons Penta or Alternate Wood Preservative

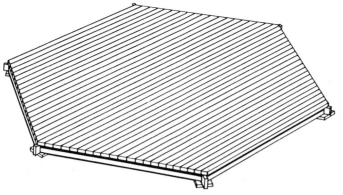

(1) A hexagonal deck approximately 12 feet square.

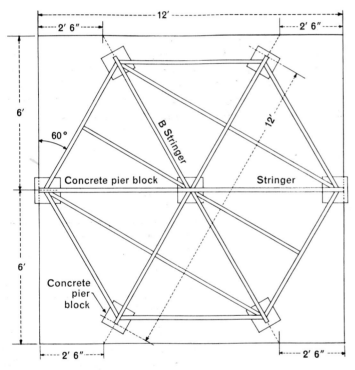

(2) Lay out deck dimensions as shown and locate piers. Excavate pier holes and level. Set the blocks and surround with gravel for drainage and support. Begin laying stringers with the central one.

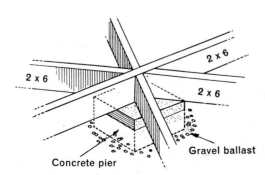

(3) Place the 12-foot center stringer first, then 6-foot ones as shown. Toe-nail all with 10-penny nails. Use temporary bracing to position stringers in proper alignment.

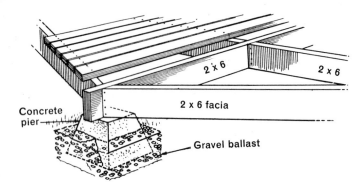

Concrete pier

Gravel ballast

2 x 6

2 x 6

2 x 6 facia

(4) Add the facia and then B stringer, as shown in (2) on page 187, and begin decking.

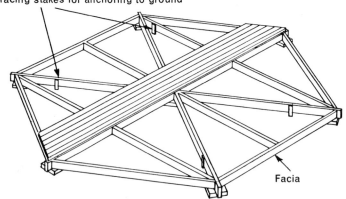

Bracing stakes for anchoring to ground

Facia

(5) Apply decking from the center over the full 12-foot stringer first. Space material with a special block or a 10-penny nail to insure even, neat design. Nail each decking to stringers with 10-penny nails. Check alignment frequently.

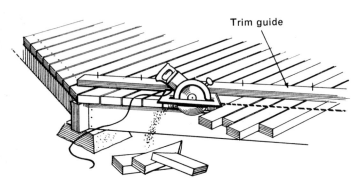

Trim guide

(6) For an even trim of edges, tack a trim guide along wood for electric saw. Allow 2-inch overhang.

MATERIAL LIST
FOR 12' x 12' DECK

Quantity	Dimension	Use	Length
1	2 x 6	Stringer	12'
6	2 x 6	Facia	6'
4	2 x 6	Stringers	6'
6	2 x 6	Inside Braces	6'
10	2 x 4	Decking	8'
10	2 x 4	Decking	10'
13	2 x 4	Decking	12'

7 Concrete Pier Blocks

4 Gallons Penta or Alternate Wood Preservative

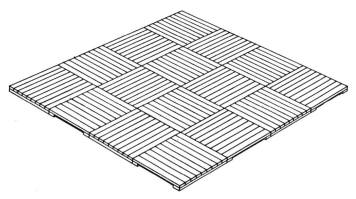

(1) Completed parquet decking has a handsome, tailored look. It is made of 3-foot squares of wood fitted together.

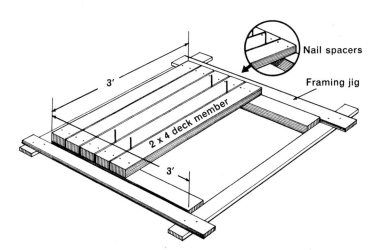

(2) Build a framing jig of light wood with an inside dimension 3 feet square. Precut 144 pieces of 2 x 4 lumber each 3 feet long, then assemble as shown. If wood is in contact with ground, it should be insect-resistant or specially treated.

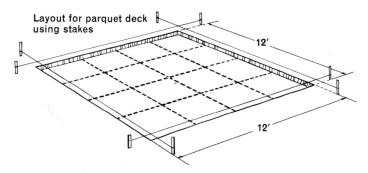

(3) Using the jig, assemble 16 parquet squares. Allow a ⅞-inch space between the parallel deck members. Nail each end of the deck with two countersunk 10-penny nails.

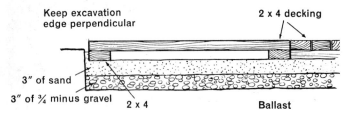

Keep excavation
edge perpendicular

2 x 4 decking

3" of sand

3" of ¾ minus gravel

2 x 4

Ballast

Cross section of parquet deck

(4) Lay out deck site with stakes and line as shown in previous drawing, then excavate to depth of 6 inches. Keep edge of site level and square, perpendicular, then fill with 3 inches of gravel not more than ¾ inch in size. Cover with 3 inches of sand and add parquet sections.

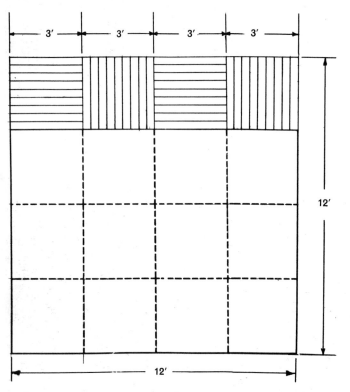

(5) Lay parquets firmly in place, alternating their direction, for design. When all have been laid, fill outside edges of excavation with sand to prevent shifting. Parquet sections can be toe-nailed together for rigidity.

MATERIAL LIST
FOR 12' x 12' DECK

Quantity	Dimension	Use	Length
32	2 x 4	Nailing Cleats	3'
144	2 x 4	Decking	3'
38 cu. ft. Sand			
38 cu. ft. Gravel			
3 Gallons Penta or Alternate Wood Preservative			

Not actually very large, this redwood deck suggests space, serenity, and order. California Redwood Association

Two types of decks. The land slopes from the street, right, to the house. A parking deck makes that portion usable without destroying the naturalness of the lot. A covered family deck, left, offers outside living space. Richard A. Campbell, A.I.A.

A deck adds to the space and livability of this mountain cabin. The fencing is particularly good-looking.

A deck that extends a patio by being built over a slope. Strybing Arboretum. Thomas D. Church, L.A.

A small deck or ledge, called an *engawa*, faces an entry to increase space and offer a place for plantings. Residence of Mr. and Mrs. Arthur Shapiro. Jocelyn Domela, L.A.

A deck can be a raised walkway joined to a lot of steps. A simple railing makes the walkway seem larger than it is.

Parquet design is effectively combined with straight boards. Strybing Arboretum. Thomas D. Church, L.A.

Concrete forming round piers with detachable metal forms. These are fastened top and bottom with straps. Another possibility is fiber-board tubing.

Concrete piers should be reinforced with ½-inch steel rods. The number required depends on the size and height of piers and the local building code. Rods are being set in a common trench of concrete because of possible earthquake damage.

Footings can be made of precast concrete pyramids or poured on the site, as were these. The purpose of footings is to keep wood from direct contact with soil to prevent decay and insect infestation. Uprights are held in place through toenails to blocks of wood set in the footings. Richard A. Campbell, A.I.A.

This drain is simply a length of plastic pipe that carries run-off from a moist area. It will be faced and buried later.

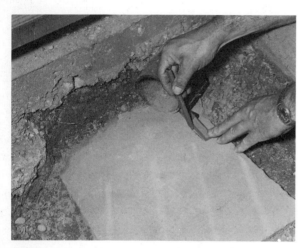

Facing a drain. A concrete pad is poured at the bottom, then the area is squared, and a place for a wooden form is marked on the concrete.

The wooden form is built in position. It is leveled, then filled with concrete mix.

The completed drain opening. The concrete will be extended to form a curbing.

Attractive drain system on the edge of a lawn. Fairly elaborate but appearing beautifully simple. Garden of Mr. and Mrs. Montgomery Fisher

A good way to measure and cut piers and beams, laying out several, marking them, and cutting all at one time.

Built-in posts for decking. On left, 2 x 4 with 1 x 2 center. On right, 2 x 2s with an open center for a lighter look.

In most cases, joists are made of smaller lumber than beams, but in this case forward joists are made of the same 4 x 6 timbers because extra weight is required.

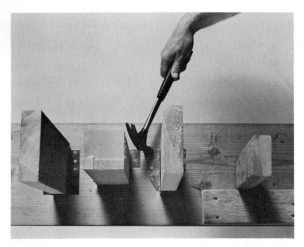

When joists are mounted flush with a beam they should be supported with a 2 x 4 cleat or with the new metal hangers, since toenailing is not reliable.

Metal hangers secure joists to beams (when flush, as these are).

For maximum strength and rigidity, railings can be secured to deck beams by bolts. Put washers at both ends to prevent compression of wood.

Timber secured to concrete column by bolts set in a metal plate cast in the concrete. A good way to attach timber to concrete.

A good idea is shown here, a railing that doubles as a seat and keeps the dominant feeling of level planes. Garden of Mr. and Mrs. Arthur Shapiro. Jocelyn Domela, L.A.

Two views of deck seen in previous photograph. (Top) The deck is simply constructed of planking set on 4 x 4 supports for strength. (Bottom) Notice how seats are mounted to the beams with bolts.

Good railing made of 2 x 6 lumber for top rail and uprights, and one 3 x 3 in the center. Below, detail. Richard A. Campbell, A.I.A.

Railing secured with metal in simple, effective, and beautiful design. Sea World

Railings specially cut to fit the parts closely and well. Workmanship is exquisite. U.C.L.A.

A tailored railing along one edge of a concrete walk. Residence of Mr. and Mrs. George Mangan

An unusual low railing with angled metal supports and a mitred surface. Handsome along the edge of low bridge-deck. Strybing Arboretum. Thomas D. Church, L.A.

10

Other Garden Structures

Recreation Areas, Shelters for Shade, and Work Centers

Auxiliary structures are wise investments. The time and money spent building them returns regular dividends in utility, convenience, and beauty. Among the more desirable are recreation centers, shade areas, gazebos, pergolas, other out-buildings, and work centers. Sandboxes and playhouses delight children, and coldframes are almost essential for serious gardeners.

Sandboxes

With crowded streets and distant playgrounds, home play centers make more sense than ever, and especially if your backyard is open and dry. Any full yard can become a part-time play center, but a planned area concentrates wear and tear, preserves the surrounding yard, and gets the greatest use. A place designed only for young children will lose its function in a few years, unless a new generation takes over, whereas a place planned with forethought for easy modification can continue to be used.

The most readily maintained play area is separated from yard and garden, but it should not give children a feeling of isolation. Hence low fences and hedges are more suitable than high walls. The area should be large enough to provide room for several children—an 8 x 10 area is the smallest practical space. Adjoining plants can be fenced off with lattice or wire. Young children are quite destructive, and even raised beds just seem to invite them to climb.

Include a variety of surfaces: grass for contact sports, dirt for digging, and a paved area. Small children will use paving for tricycles, mud pies, and finger painting, and older ones will use it for shuffle-board, dancing, and other activities. Little children are satisfied with small amounts of water, a portable pool or a lawn sprinkler; older children will usually want a swimming pool—which is a project outside of the play area proper and one that demands professional installation.

A sandbox is essential for young children, and the larger the box, the better. Big boxes invite participation, and a child with friends beside him remains at home. A 2 x 4-foot box is the smallest you should build; one 6 x 8 feet is big enough to satisfy half a dozen kids. The sand should be at least a foot deep.

The box can be permanent or temporary. Many parents build permanent ones of brick and concrete, and in later years convert them to pools with recirculating pumps and water plants. For a temporary box, decay-resistant wood or thoroughly painted softwood is most satisfactory. Two-inch lumber makes the sturdiest sides. The depth should be 18 to 24 inches (made from 2 x 12s and 2 x 6s, for example), the corners reinforced with 2 x 4s or galvanized pipe. Be sure the lumber is smooth, well sanded, and free of splinters. A galvanized facing further reduces that danger. Boxes can be sunk if the location is dry and well drained but should be built aboveground in damp soils.

Swings, slides, log structures

To increase the appeal of a play area, add some recreational equipment. You can buy various items but you can build your own, including some not commercially available and made from common objects. Tires are an example. The traditional tire-on-a-rope is still popular, and tires suggest other structures. For example, insert four eyebolts into the casing, attach nylon ropes to each, then hang the tire horizontally. It will hold three small children, who can twist until the ropes are wound tight. As they unwind, the tire becomes a merry-go-round. Or remove the tread from half a tire, leaving the outer edge or bead intact. The bottom, where the tread remains, becomes a safe seat for a child, and the beading above is the point at which you attach ropes.

Build a slide from a 4 x 8 sheet of ¼-inch hardboard. Bend the sheet into a U-shaped trough. Support the edges with 2 x 4s and set 2 x 4 legs at the ends. Place cross braces directly under the U. The factory surface may be slippery enough but a good waxing will give a better ride. The steeper the incline, the faster the descent.

Many small children are fascinated by structures made from peeled logs piled lengthwise, fastened together at varying heights, with the base set firmly in the ground. Children can climb over, walk along, or jump from different levels. Where there is space, strong peeled trees with side branches and forks can be set upright in concrete for children to climb upon and explore. For security and permanence, set the logs in concrete well below ground level. Be sure all wood is coated with chemical protection before it is buried. A recreational area in the John Baldwin Park, in Concord, California, includes imaginative variations on logs for play material, as our illustrations show.

Playhouses

Children have always liked a playhouse, transforming it vicariously into a hut, a castle, a hospital, a space ship, a dungeon. Perhaps the smallest adequate size is 4 x 4, but you can change the dimensions and later add extensions. Let your youngsters participate in the choice. Plans for simple structures are available from manufacturers of plywood and hardwood material, and unusual features of decoration can be added as you go.

Treehouses are always good, and now it is not even necessary to own a tree. I saw one elegant structure set atop a pole in a Eugene, Oregon, backyard and found another nearby made of a circle of eight poles. The hollow shaft in that one offered a way up and down. At the top I found two floors, a balcony, and a Japanese roof.

Lawn sports

Set an area aside for adults: Croquet, golf, shuffleboard, and even tennis are possibilities, and you will discover they are games teen-agers take to readily. Shuffleboard demands a hard surface; the other sports, unless played very frequently, will not seriously damage an established and well-cared-for lawn. Paved areas, especially blacktop, can be unsightly and should be carefully placed in relation to the rest of the grounds. If possible, let existing pavements, such as a garage court or parking place, double as a game area.

It is commonly assumed that considerable space is needed, but compromises are always possible, as these suggestions show:

CROQUET. An official court is 36 x 72 feet, but the game can be played successfully on a court half that size. Be sure the surface is level. Packed dirt is acceptable, but grass is better (and move the wickets occasionally to reduce wear). Lawn bowling and other games can be played on the same surface.

GOLF.   You can build either a putting green or miniature course with three or four holes in very little space. A 15 x 4-foot area of the yard will suffice. Seed it with a tight-growing lawn mix.

SHUFFLEBOARD.   Although the official court is 6 x 52 feet, a 30-foot depth can provide plenty of fun. Use any concrete mixture that can be carefully leveled and troweled smooth. For the tally sections at the ends set brass or plastic numbers in the concrete. Include a shelter at one end to hold equipment.

TENNIS.   A full-sized court requires 60 x 120 feet, but games such as hand tennis can be played in spaces as small as 16 x 40. The official badminton court requires 20 x 44 feet, but the game can be played in an area 10 x 20. A Ping-Pong table is theoretically demountable, but it is difficult to put one up and take down frequently, and most remain up during the summer season. Place yours in an area where it can stay up during the summer months.

Garden shelters

Places for shade can be attached to a house, such as permanent porches or temporary awnings, or made free-standing, such as gazebos and pergolas. A gazebo can be defined as "a pavilion or summerhouse on a site affording an enjoyable view." A summerhouse is a simple, often rustic structure in a park or garden, intended to provide a shady, cool sitting place. A pergola, in contrast, is "an arbor or trellis treated architecturally" and has come to imply a walk shaded or partly shaded by vines grown on supports on both sides or by overhead lathing.

Contemporary garden shelters are generally rectangular or square. More complex styles, as in some of the gazebos illustrated, are used for dramatic effect. The typical nineteenth-century summerhouse was polygonal or round. Roofs may be flat or sloping, gabled or peaked or pyramidal. If the roof is to be watertight, it should be sloped to run off the rain. When the design becomes complicated or heavy, professional help may be needed to make sure that structural loads are properly supported and distributed. Plan in advance for water pipes and electric connections so that both can be buried to keep the landscape clear.

You can choose between metal and wood to build structures as diverse as a simple post-and-beam arbor and a complex full-weather shelter. However, metal is commonly joined by professional welding or bolting; wood is obviously the more practical material for the layman.

SUPPORTS.   A post-and-beam design is suitable for many arbors and pergolas, though architects tell me there is a tendency to build them of too light material. Assured strength depends upon supports of the right size. As with decks, 4 x 4 timbers are generally adequate. The footings can range from tamped earth or poured concrete to the poured and precast types recommended for decking. Posts set directly in the ground should be of a resistant wood (all-heart redwood is good); footings set above ground level on concrete may be of softwood.

Uprights are often set in the ground and held firm by tamped earth, but poured concrete increases reliability and strength. Make sure the posts are plumb on two sides; if concrete is added, brace them temporarily. Post depth depends on soil and wind conditions, 36 inches being normally adequate for an 8-foot structure.

Beams support the rafters; the greatest strength derives from those set directly above the posts. The rafters can support roofing or can stand uncovered. Open rafters create broken shade and interesting patterns and can be used as a trellis. Cut usually from 2 x 4s or 2 x 6s, they can be fastened above the beams, notched to fit around them, or set flush and held by cleats or metal hangers.

ROOFING. Various materials can be used for roofing—shake, shingle, reed fencing, and even screening. Whatever you choose should harmonize with the understructure in color and texture. If you like the contrast of shadow and sunlight, try lath, which tempers the wind without eliminating circulation. Lath can be almost anything from 2 x 3 strips to ½ x 3 battens. Strips wider than 5 or 6 inches seem out of scale on most buildings.

A popular roof pattern for warm areas is the eggcrate, an open design of wood crossed at right angles. This is most simply made of long lumber laid in one direction with short pieces attached crosswise; a stronger crate employs long lumber in both directions, the members dadoed for accurate fit—i.e., set into rectangular, flat-bottomed grooves. The first system requires only the simplest tools; the other can be done best with a table or radial saw.

PLYWOOD SIDING. Most shelters have at least one wall solid or louvered for privacy and protection against wind. The wall can be built on 2 x 4 or 4 x 4 uprights set 4 feet apart, but where gusty winds are apt to occur, increase the wall strength with cross-bracing or additional uprights. Plywood is a common choice for solid siding because it is inexpensive and easily and quickly attached. One sheet cover a 4 x 8-foot section.

The choice of surface ranges from smooth to rough, with a variety of textures, groove designs, and stains. For its weight, plywood is stronger than steel, rustproof, and has less expansion and contraction than conventional lumber. Be sure to specify exterior or marine grades for outdoor use: other varieties may warp.

Plywood panels are graded according to the quality of the face veneer (the exposed surface). There are four categories: A—near perfect with no defects, although neat patches are permitted; B—small defects but generally uniform and good; C—knotholes and splits permitted; D—rough surface with wide splits and large holes. A and B grades are recommended if a surface is exposed. C grade can be used when it will be hidden. D panels are never used for construction.

Both surfaces are graded. The finest panels are graded A–A, and exterior construction panels are graded from A–A to A–C, depending on whether one or both surfaces are to be exposed. Marine panels, among the finest available, are commonly sold only in A–A and A–B grades. All are sold in a variety of thicknesses from ⅛ inch to ¾, the best for siding being ⅜ and ⅝ inch.

SCREENS. Screening can be used in place of solid siding to provide ventilation, an open view, and protection from insects. Of the many screens available, fiberglass and aluminum are recommended for garden shelters because they are rustproof and fireproof. The costs are about the same, less than forty cents a linear foot, and both are available in several widths. A 4-foot width is normally used, since the uprights are spaced that way, but occasionally widths up to 84 inches are required.

Screens are usually available in seven colors—gray, charcoal, green, aqua, bronze, gold, and white. The darker colors make for greater visibility, the lighter colors for privacy and coolness, as they reflect more light and heat on the outer side. If intense sun is a problem, as in a due-south exposure, try louvered aluminum screening. The openings are small enough to block most insects and angled against the sun without reducing ventilation.

Save scraps of screen for repairs. Holes in aluminum screening can be repaired by weaving new strands over the old. Small holes in fiberglass can be repaired with dabs of waterproof glue. Larger holes in fiberglass screens should be repaired by gluing patches over the area. No screen can withstand the onslaught of children without bulging, but you can reduce the prospect of damage at the bottom of doors with decorative shields. Buy ready-made aluminum shields or make your own from plywood.

Lath houses

An efficient and attractive way of growing many plants, particularly those that need part shade, is under lathing. This is a favorite of gardeners in regions of long dry summers. A good lath house furnishes broken shade and some humidity control. Ferns, begonias, astilbes, caladiums, and impatiens are among the interesting plants that respond well to such treatment. A strong supporting framework can be made of 2 x 4s or 4 x 6s, and a generally adequate one of lighter lumber. If moisture is a problem, the roof should be slanted and the lath laid diagonally, with a metal gutter at the base to catch water.

The lath pattern determines the kind of sun control. A standard design—i.e., strips separated by openings of equal width—controls morning and evening sun. One- or 2-foot squares, alternated checkerboard fashion, are effective against midday sun. Lath of two widths— ½ inch and 2 inches, for example—spaced one and a half to twice the width of each lath, or standard lath alternated above and below the rafter, offers good all-day control.

Portable lath panels have many garden uses. Convenient, manageable frames are 3 x 6 or 4 x 8 feet. They can be placed against fences to protect seedlings, raised over picnic areas to shade guests, or combined as a screen for privacy. Their utility will match your ingenuity. For framing, take 2 x 2s or 2 x 3s, reinforce the corners with plywood, and use 1 x 2 batten strips, rather than standard lath, for extra strength.

Work centers

Every gardener needs a work center. It can be, and often is, only a picnic bench or a small corner of the garage, but when it is tailored for the work to be done it creates far better and happier gardening. The basic components include orderly storage for tools, soils, mulches, and chemicals, and a workbench for potting and mixing. Devoted gardeners will also want growing areas, indoors or out, for starting seeds, nursing injured plants, etc. In northern climates, bins or racks for overwintering dormant tender bulbs and tubers are a great help.

The best location is within easy reach of house, yard, and drive, yet not obtruding on the visual and recreational aspects of the property. Behind the garage, a section of the service area, or along a back fence are usual locations. Bear in mind that the place should be neither too warm nor too cool, out of prevailing winds, within carrying distance of the car, and—since a work center grows as your garden grows— spacious enough for expansion.

STORAGE. If you need only a small storage unit, a ready-made locker may be suitable. Some are just right to stand beneath the eaves. When more storage and a worktable are needed, you can consider easy-to-assemble metal structures, the type popular with mobile home-owners. If you build your workroom, take advantage of the outside house or garage walls. Sometimes, too, the overhang there is such that a narrow attached storage center will not need its own roof.

Good tools need weather protection. A shed will hold and protect most garden tools. Organize hand tools on shelves. Provide wide doors for mowers, fertilizer spreaders, and wheelbarrows. Keep fertilizers in bins, or if you use small amounts, in covered plastic buckets. Poisons should be stored in locked and childproof compartments. You can save time by bolting a surplus metal case to one wall. You can custom-build cabinets from ½-inch plywood. For a childproof latch, drill a hole through the top of a plywood door. Add a loose-fitting nail to the hole, then cut the top flush so it cannot be lifted with the fingers. Children cannot release the catch yet you can release it quickly with a magnet.

Storage bins can be made in several ways. Perhaps the easiest is simply to set several metal or plastic garbage cans on a wheeled platform. Or build square boxes open at the top, low enough to fit beneath the workbench. Add wheels, and they can be pulled out easily as you work. Or build a three-section bin below the bench. Or try tip-out bins. You can make them with ¾-inch plywood, facing the front with any lumber that matches, or is painted to match, the storage center. Bins can easily be supported by a galvanized pipe set through holes near the bottoms on which the bins can pivot.

Occasionally, portable storage helps. A woman in Minnesota had her husband build a cabinet on wheels. It is 4 feet high, 2 feet wide, and 20 inches deep, with compartments for broom, rake, and shovel, and shelves for everything from pots to fertilizers. She pulls the cabinet along behind her as she works and estimates it saves a mile of walking every week.

WORKBENCH.   For any serious gardener a workbench is indispensable. A small one can be attached to a wall with 2 x 4s topped with ½-inch plywood or with 1 x 6 or 2 x 6 boards. The work surface should be at a convenient height, usually waist level, i.e., between 32 and 36 inches. Some people prefer a higher level, at which they can work either standing or seated on a stool. The outer edge can be supported by 2 x 4s angled to the wall or by legs. If the bench is outdoors, be sure to put concrete slabs below the legs to keep them dry and to prevent settling, and if you add a collar of water, the bench will be ant-proof.

SHELVES.   Use 1 x 12-inch lumber or ½-inch plywood for shelving. Cut each piece squarely and choose a mounting that is unobtrusive. The quickest: preformed metal brackets common in garages. The simplest: 1 x 2-inch cleats nailed to the uprights; the faces hidden with molding strips. A less obvious mounting uses angle irons in the rear as the front edges are held with nails through the uprights.

Adjustable shelving is better. You can make your own by drilling holes in the uprights, adding dowels to support the shelves. Ready-made shelves of this kind are generally easier to level, and the best are metal strips that nail or screw to the uprights. Small clips or 12-inch brackets fit to slots in the strips. A newer type features short U-shaped metal holders with attached nails. These are fastened to the uprights at points where you want shelves.

Coldframes

A coldframe is invaluable. The simplest consists of little more than four walls and a transparent roof. In dry climates the roof can be flat, but elsewhere it must slope to carry off rain or snow. The structure can be of any size you prefer, but if you plan to use glass, find the sash first, then build to fit. The smallest practical size is 2 x 4 feet. Frames of 3 x 4 and 4 x 6 are popular because commercial glass sash comes in these sizes.

The sides of the frame should extend 15 to 24 inches above-ground, built of resistant wood (redwood, cedar, cypress) or of soft-woods treated with a preservative, such as copper naphthenate. Planks can be joined at the ends without extra support, but the frame will be sturdier with bracing, for which 2 x 4s or 2 x 2s driven into the ground are adequate.

The bottom of the frame should be below ground level. In cold areas place it 6 to 30 inches below the frost line, including 4 inches of gravel for drainage. Potted plants can be placed upon this. The sides of the frame are generally erected after the interior has been dug.

Tops can be made of glass or plastic. I prefer plastic because it is unbreakable, inexpensive, and easily replaced. I make my frames of 2 x 2 softwoods, the corners braced with angle irons or plywood. Top and bottom are covered with plastic pulled tight and secured with lath. Where snow is a problem, add wire mesh to help support the load.

You can increase the effectiveness of a frame with heat. If you prefer soil instead of gravel, add heating tape to the soil itself. If you use gravel, install light bulbs above the frame—50-watt bulbs spaced about 1 foot apart. Be sure to order waterproof sockets and well-insulated wiring. Include 10- or 15-amp fuses. The heat can be controlled by a thermostat or by the number of bulbs.

SHELTERS AND STORAGE
(Courtesy of California Redwood Association)

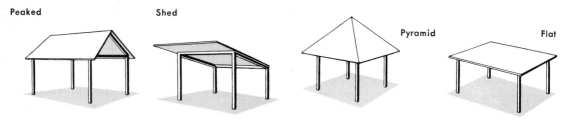

Peaked   Shed   Pyramid   Flat

The intended purpose of a garden shelter determines its design and location. Only in regions of long dry seasons is a flat roof practical; elsewhere the roof must be sloped to shed rain.

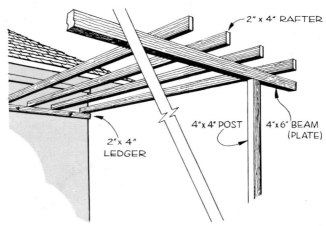

2" x 4" RAFTER

2" x 4" LEDGER

4"x 4" POST

4"x 6" BEAM (PLATE)

Some shelters can be attached to existing buildings by a modification of the basic post-and-beam construction. Here the far ends of rafters rest directly on a ledger strip fastened to the building.

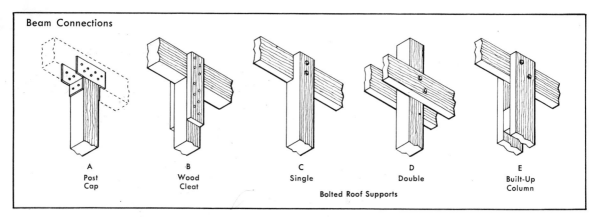

Beam Connections

A	B	C	D	E
Post Cap	Wood Cleat	Single	Double	Built-Up Column

Bolted Roof Supports

Beams support the rafters, giving rigidity to a structure. Several methods of construction are possible. The best bearing is achieved when the beam is placed directly upon the post. A patented cap (A) is useful where the beam is the same width as the post.

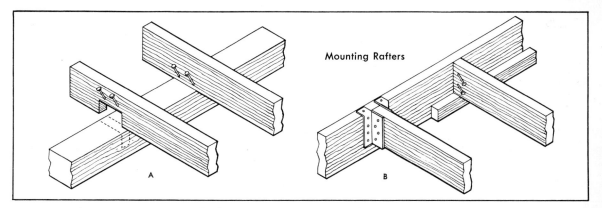

Rafters support the finished roof or may be used alone to create an open pattern. Four common methods of installation are: (A) notched or simply nailed on above the beam and (B) set flush by a patented hanger or a wood ledger strip.

The roof of a shelter can be one of its most interesting features. An open design permits the play of sun and shadow. Blocked patterns are made with rafters in one direction and shorter pieces at right angles.

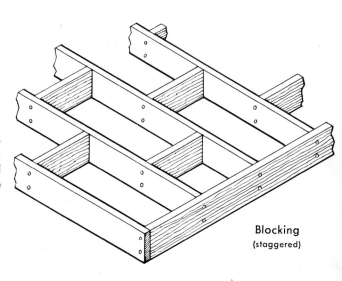

Blocking
(staggered)

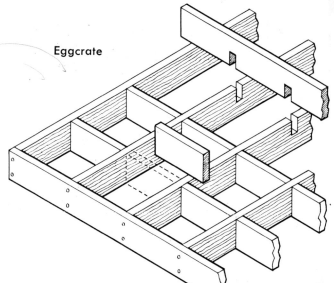

Eggcrate

Eggcrate design can be made with notched lumber or with short pieces set flush.

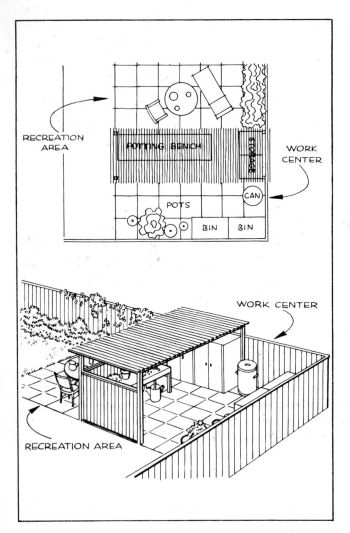

An unobtrusive location for a work center is often beside a fence or behind a garage or carport. Here a recreation place and a work center are combined.

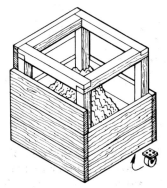

A simple storage idea. A self-contained bin with casters can roll in and out beneath a bench.

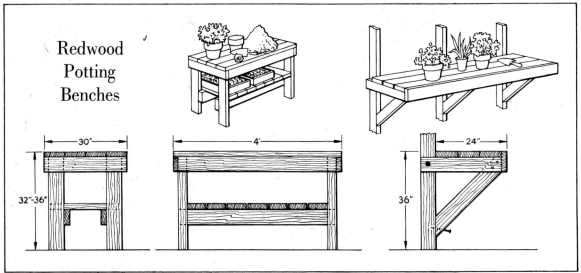

Redwood Potting Benches

Although a complete work area may not be possible, you may find room for a bench that is either free-standing or attached to a wall. The top should be of a convenient height and wide enough for most work.

Two-story playhouse 7½ feet high x 8 feet long, sturdy and challenging to the child's imagination. Window should be see-through plastic. (Plan available at about $1.00 from Masonite Corporation.)

A play place should include a sandbox and readymade toys. This sand area is sunk; when children are older, it can be converted into a shallow pool. Braemar Homes. Armstrong and Sharfman, L.A.

SANDBOX:

(1) Lay out the dimensions on the ground. Mark the corners with ends of pipe or wooden stakes. The pipes can be permanent corners if you like, and the wood attached with straps and screws. (2) Sandboxes can be above ground or partly sunken, depending on ground conditions, since the sand should dry quickly after rain. If sunk, excavate inside the staked area. (3) Sides of the box are made from 1 x 12 lumber joined at the corners and reinforced with 2 x 2. (This is an aboveground box.) (4) Square the corners by the rule of 3-4-5. (5) Add a top edging for safety and appearance. (6) Then add sand and children.

Arrangements and construction of peeled logs fascinate small children. For permanence, set logs in concrete. Three photos from John Baldwin Park, Concord, California. Theodore Osmundson and Associates, L.A.

A five-sided gazebo partly roofed and seating eight or more—a pleasant place in a warm garden. Garden of Dick Richards. Marc Askew, designer

An open-sided shelter creates coolness and shade and a sense of serenity. Gardens of Mr. and Mrs. Carl Pannatoni. Marc Askew, designer

A decorative canopy of rough lumber in eggcrate roofing, with solid panels above, provides a restful and focal area. Marc Askew, designer

Trellis extending from a closed patio area defines the edge of the lawn, carries the line of the patio, and gives a feeling of enclosure in a gentle way. Lloyd Bond, L.A.

Uprights carry a simple horizontal rafterwork that is rhythmic and attractive.

An airy gazebo adjoining a concrete pad. Simplicity of design emphasizes the view. Overhead latticework gives moving shadows. Garden of Mr. and Mrs. Irving Hammer, Jack Buktenica, L.A.

Openwork redwood over a gallery protects the large windows from glare in summer but admits light and warmth in winter, also ties the house to the landscape. California Redwood Association. Morley Baer photo. David Leaf, architect

A solid roof for all-weather protection over the dining center, and an open-rafter design for visual interest and some shade. Braemar Homes. Armstrong and Sharfman, L.A.

Open-rafter construction casts this pleasant pattern on an entry and keeps the sun from the front door even in late afternoon. Deane Homes

Most effective simplicity—an arbor made of telephone poles with a light framework and wire above. Garden of Mr. and Mrs. Harold Hecht. Jocelyn Domela, L.A.

The effectiveness of a simple lath cover. Late afternoon rays are gently reduced. May-fair Homes

In gazebos and pergolas, diagonal bracing is often needed to help distribute weights from roof and rafter members. Upright timbers must be strong. Marc Askew, designer

Bamboo is a good overhead cover in mild and dry regions. Los Angeles County Arboretum

An interesting variation of lath, cut from a single board, with a rafter interwoven above and below. A similar effect could be made with separate strips. Los Angeles County Arboretum

Privacy for a window on the street side—a screen of lath hung from the roof and painted to contrast with the rough-textured wood of the house. Courtesy of Mr. and Mrs. Montgomery Fisher

Construction detail: The post is capped, the roof is plastic. Strybing Arboretum

Construction detail: Beams set flush should be supported with cleats or with metal hangers (as here). Strybing Arboretum

Here a face plate has been bolted to the building, then the beams attached with metal hangers. Mayfair Homes

Beams can also be attached to uprights by bolts. Two uprights here hold a 2 x 12 beam. The 2 x 4 crosspiece is for bracing. Mayfair Homes

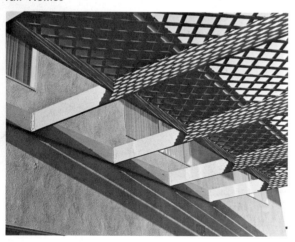

A series of supports are crossed and bolted to 2 x 3 uprights. Marc Askew, designer

Beams can also be mounted directly at the roof line. This beam has been cut to fit around the overhang and fastened from behind. Mayfair Homes

Roof beam attached to a concrete column through a metal plate set in the concrete. The laminated beam is bolted to the plate. Richard A. Campbell, A.I.A.

Here metal arms lift the upright above the concrete. This method keeps the foot of the lumber dry, thwarts insects, and prevents wood-to-concrete contact.

Another method of attaching uprights: Concrete post is cast when patio is constructed, and uprights are bolted to it. These uprights are also lifted above the concrete.

The rear (driveway side) of a potting-storage facility. The front opens to the garden. One bin is for mulch, which can be dumped in the driveway, shoveled into the bin on this side, and taken out on the garden side. Saves a lot of wheelbarrowing. Slanted lids have plastic covering to shed rain. Courtesy of Western Wood Products Association. Chandler Fairbank, L.A.

A handsome work and storage center in the garden behind the house. Garden of Robert Krohn

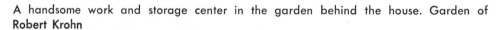

A concrete pad was poured; now the framework of 2 x 4s is under way.

Work-counter height is set with a 2 x 4 and carefully leveled.

This work center is divided into three parts, each framed with a 2 x 4. One will provide working space; the others, storage. Roof overhang offers sufficient protection, so that additional roofing is not required.

Bins are built separately to go under the counter, then fitted in place (but not attached) before the structure is completed.

A bin is made of ¾- or ½-inch plywood. Photo shows how the sections are reinforced. Use waterproof glue and galvanized nails.

Bins will swing on this galvanized pipe. Flanged ends will be secured to the 2 x 4 uprights.

Pipe can be supported by a 2 x 4 or other arrangement.

Walls are reinforced with 2 x 4s, since shelving will require strength.

Adding the wall siding—in this case 1 x 12 rough-textured cedar boards.

The storage center completed except for doors.

A simple and effective lath house. Benches inside hold a variety of plants. Lath patterns reduce sunlight and help control humidity. Garden of Dr. and Mrs. Francis E. Howard

Lattice on supports of galvanized pipe set in concrete in the ground and secured to the wood through flanges. Garden of Mr. and Mrs. George Mangan

234

Other parts of the same structure (preceding photo). It has the same effect of a lath house on the hillside vegetation and accommodates an old tree.

(1) Excavate to the desired size and to below the frost line. Then build the walls as panels to be fitted together in the hole. I use 1 x 12 pecky cedar—inexpensive and insect-resistant. (2) Rear panel is fitted into place. Level it by digging earth from the bottom. Thoroughly reinforce with 2 x 4s. (3) Front panel is built the same way, then leveled. (4) End sections are similarly constructed. When all panels are fitted and leveled, fasten them with 16-penny galvanized nails. All edges should be square; all panels level and plumb.

5

(5) Edges are faced with 1 x 4 cedar to make a flat, neat surface for the top frames. (6) Top frame is made from 2 x 2 wood (in this case cut from a 2 x 4). The lighter wood reduces weight without sacrificing strength. (7) After top frames are assembled, they should be covered. Glass can be used as panes or sash; for strength I use corrugated translucent plastic attached with roofing tacks. (8) The best coldframes are weatherproof. All cracks should be covered. Here the side edges have a 1 x 4 facing of cedar. The inside can be further weatherproofed with asphalt building paper. Fill the bottom of the frame with a ¾-inch layer of gravel.

7

A general storage center at ground level and under a deck. Lockable, it holds all sorts of garden tools and materials.

Acknowledgments

A special "thank you" to my wife, Peggy, for help with sections of this book and to Daniel T. Walden for technical and general assistance. Gratitude is also expressed to the following architects, landscape architects, designers, business firms, associations, and public gardens for having permitted the taking of photographs or the use of drawings, charts, or other materials prepared by them:

American Plywood Association
Tacoma, Wash.

Armstrong and Sharfman, L.A.
Los Angeles, Calif.

Marc Askew (designer)
Sacramento, Calif.

John Baldwin Park
Concord, Calif.

Lloyd Bond, L.A.
Eugene, Ore.

Braemar Homes (developers)
Los Angeles, Calif.

Jack Buktenica, L.A.
Los Angeles, Calif.

California Redwood Association
San Francisco, Calif.

Richard A. Campbell, A.I.A.
Portland, Ore.

Thomas D. Church, L.A.
San Francisco, Calif.

Joseph Copp, L.A.
Los Angeles, Calif.

Corolite Division
Coronado Manufacturing Co.
Long Beach, Calif.

Deane Homes (developers)
Thousand Oaks, Calif.

Jocelyn Domela, L.A.
Beverly Hills, Calif.

Eckbo, Dean, Austin and Williams, L.A.
Los Angeles and San Francisco, Calif.

Eriksson, Peters & Thoms, L.A.
Pasadena, Calif.

Chandler Fairbank, A.S.L.A.
Portland, Ore.

Lawrence Halprin and Associates, L.A.
San Francisco, Calif.

Holiday Inn
Gallup, N. Mex.

Los Angeles County Arboretum
Los Angeles, Calif.

Lytton Center
Oakland, Calif.

Masonite Corporation
Dover, Ohio

Mayfair Homes (Westlake Village) (developers)
Thousand Oaks, Calif.

Bob McCabe (artist)
Sacramento, Calif.

National Audubon Society
New York, N. Y.

Nut Tree Restaurant
Nut Tree, Calif.

Theodore Osmundson and Associates, L.A.
San Francisco, Calif.

Portland Cement Association
Skokie, Ill.

La Posada Inn
La Paz, Baja Sur, Mexico

Sea World
San Diego, Calif.

Strybing Arboretum
San Francisco, Calif.

University of California at Los Angeles
   (U.C.L.A.)
Los Angeles, Calif.

Western Wood Products Association
Portland, Ore.

Hilda Wiedmann (designer)
Paradise, Calif.

Gratitude is also expressed to the following owners of private gardens:

Mr. and Mrs. A. Bloom

Dr. and Mrs. Chui

Mr. John Dutro

Mr. and Mrs. Montgomery Fisher

Mr. and Mrs. David Foster

Mr. and Mrs. Irving Hammer

Mr. and Mrs. Harold Hecht

Dr. and Mrs. Francis E. Howard

Mr. and Mrs. Robert Jones

Mr. and Mrs. Robert Krohn

Mr. and Mrs. George Mangan

Mr. and Mrs. John Moehlmann

Mr. and Mrs. Carl Panattoni

Mrs. Gretchen Plechner

Mr. and Mrs. Arthur J. Priestly

Mrs. Sally Reed

Mr. Dick Richards

Mr. and Mrs. William Robinson

Mr. and Mrs. Arthur Shapiro

Mrs. Emil Steinegger

Index